Growing Together
Horsham's Town Allotments

Author's Pen

Worthing Road, Horsham, West Sussex. RH12 1TD

Copyright Notice

Author's Pen

Other works by the same author

Secret Horsham, by Maggie Weir-Wilson, published by Amberley Publishing, published 15th August 2019, ISBN 978-1445686455

St Leonard's Forest: A Landscape History, published by Author's Pen, second edition published 2021, print ISBN 978-1838343606, e-book ISBN 9781838343613

Foreword

I have been involved with the management of allotments for almost thirty years, initially as part of my role within HDC and subsequently taking on my own plot fifteen years ago. At one time I was responsible for managing, inspecting and maintaining the waiting lists for eight sites – this took up a lot of my working week. In 2013, I was tasked with encouraging each site to become self-managed. The first, Clarence Road, formed a society in 2014.

Some sites were sceptical that self-management would prove successful, however I am sure they would all agree that it has resulted in many benefits such as a better maintained site and the holding of social events. The availability of grants has also helped Horsham's allotments to secure funding for sheds, mowers, toilets etc., which would not have been possible if the sites were still managed by the council.

Allotments form an important part of Horsham's history, yet there has been very little written about them in the past and not a lot of easily accessible information is available. It was therefore a delight to learn that Maggie was planning to write a book recording the past history and present status of our sites.

We are fortunate in Horsham to have so many statutory allotment sites, and it is reassuring that the future provision is secured by the requirement that the larger housing developers have to provide new sites as part of the Planning Guidelines. The popularity of allotments has wavered over the years, and it is encouraging that the health and wellbeing benefits (already known to existing plot holders) are now widely recognised and they are no longer viewed as just a cheap way of growing food. We are also seeing an increase in younger families taking on plots as they wish to know exactly where their food is coming from and that it has not been modified. It also gives them the opportunity to grow unusual foods not readily available or affordable in shops.

This book provides a background to the chequered history of our sites, how we have nearly lost some along the way and how some have moved, sometimes just around the corner, to accommodate housing or other needs. It not only tells us about the history of the allotment movement and our own individual sites, but Maggie has visited and spoken to tenants at each site and recorded their stories and memories.

It's a fascinating read and if you don't already have an allotment, it will certainly encourage you to think about taking one on!

Lynda Cheeseman
HDC Parks & Countryside Officer, 1994-2020

Acknowledgements

In order to write a book about Horsham's allotments I have had to rely on the willingness of many allotment society committee members and plot holders to show me around their allotment site, allow me to take photos, share with me their memories and stories, and talk about the basics of running an allotment site, in times of pandemic and afterwards. I therefore have many people to thank from each allotment site to thank for their patience and generosity in answering my many questions. You know who you are.

Particular thanks should go to those committee members who were kind enough to read the draft chapters about their specific allotment site to ensure I had got everything right. This was invaluable. Thank you.

Special thanks are due to Lynda Cheeseman, who previously managed allotments for Horsham District Parks Department, and who has been a constant source of information, suggestions and support. I also thank her, and John Connolly of Clarence Road allotment site for reading the first drafts, a time consuming but very necessary task that is much appreciated. Thanks, are also due to those who helped me negotiate the historic archives, both the team at West Sussex Records Office in Chichester, and Nikki Caxton, our new curator at Horsham Museum.

I would, of course, like to thank Leigh Ann Gale, botanic artist and tutor whose help and encouragement in her monthly workshops undoubtedly helped me to produce all my paintings of allotment fruit and vegetables seen at the beginning of eight chapters. For the poetry which begins the other chapters, I have only myself to blame, but with useful feedback from the Horsham Writers Circle.

Finally, thanks to Lesley Hart of Author's Pen for the task of encouraging, editing and publishing this very local Horsham book about allotments.

Contents

Introduction

Why did I want to write this book about Horsham's town allotments? I think, first and foremost, because I have enjoyed working on my own full-size allotment at the Chesworth site for over ten years now. It has been a steep learning curve as to the growing of fruit and vegetables, but also, I began wondering about my fellow allotmenteers. How long had they had an allotment? Why were they growing this or that? What brought them to this site? I then wondered how long Chesworth had been going as a site? And, what about all the other allotment sites in the centre of town? We seemed to have quite a few compared to other towns, why was that? And, of course, most fascinating was, what was going on at those other sites?

So, I had lots of questions and I was aware that not much actually gets written about specific town allotments, certainly nothing comprehensive had been written about our Horsham allotments. I had come across Paul Eustice's, *Diggers All, a history of allotments in Worthing* published in 2019 which was prompted by the move of responsibility for management of their allotments from the council to Worthing Allotment Management (WAM) and the inheritance of *several trailer loads of box files*. I was not so lucky – or unlucky – the archives on Horsham's allotments were very patchy.

I decided to just go with what I could obtain from the West Sussex Records Office in Chichester which mainly consisted of council letters and notes regarding the buying of some tracts of land for development and allotments, plus responses to petty complaints. There were a few nuggets of stories which were great and shone a light on how things have changed over the past seventy or eighty years, but many allotment sites were not mentioned. Likewise, in Horsham Museum archives were limited to some old photos and a few notes. However, my book was not to be just a history, fascinating as this was, but a celebration of our allotment sites. The people and their plots. What had happened in the past according to their memories and what was happening now would definitely be worth recording for posterity, while it was still possible.

All of the town allotments, except Hills Farm, are statutory in that they cannot be used for a different purpose, or sold, without consent from the government according to section 8 of the 1925 Allotment Act. Given that the government seems keener on houses than allotments this is another reason for recording their history and their benefit to the community while we can.

I visited all the allotments between lockdowns, in the summer of 2021, which in retrospect was not ideal for writing this book since many of the allotment sites has ceased their usual social events and were only just beginning to reinstate them in 2022. However, as far as health goes, allotments are the perfect place to be when there is a pandemic about. Demand for plots was buoyant and the waiting lists all increased – not surprisingly.

I was very grateful to the plot-holders who talked to me and were happy to be photographed, it all added to the interesting picture I have been able to build of Horsham's town allotments. Although there are many similarities between sites, there are also clearly differences. In many ways it depends on how big the site is, how active the committee is and whether there are those valuable volunteers to do the necessary maintenance tasks. Some sites are more socially proactive than others, but again this relies on a motivated committee and volunteers, plus, as I mentioned, the allotments are just recovering from the restrictive years of the pandemic.

One thing that has been developing in most of the allotment sites has been an increasing acknowledgment and respect for nature. This has encouraged a reduction in the use of pesticides and a move to more organic, sustainable practices. This includes the establishment of wildlife plots, bird and bat boxes, ponds and bug houses.

I have taken a lot of photographs as I think this helps to inform readers of what the allotments are actually like, the size of the plots and what is growing. It also celebrates our plot holders, their hard work and skill. With regard to plot holders, not everyone wanted their photo taken or name shown so I have respected their wishes, and not all were as forthcoming as others with their memories and stories. Many just wanted to work on their plots in peace and this was fine. It has meant, of course, that I couldn't put in what I was not told, so inevitably there will be gaps.

I have recorded what I managed to obtain, another author might produce something different and add to the Horsham allotment story. I have in the first three chapters set the allotment movement in its historical context, which is interesting and helps to understand why we in Britain have allotments in the first place. With regard to the specific Horsham allotments and where relevant I have started with the 1840 Tithe Map which shows the first allotments rented to the Horsham Labourers' Friend Society, only three sites, but regarded by the society as a sort of food bank, keeping the local labourers out of mischief and well fed.

After the first three historical chapters, I look at each of the eleven town allotments in alphabetical order. Hills Farm is of necessity just a small chapter as it is being absorbed by the cemetery and is no longer available to new plot holders. Readers will see that I have indulged my hobbies of botanic art and poetry in that each chapter is either preceded with a poem or watercolour. It gives me great pleasure to enable these to be seen. Hopefully you will feel they are appropriate and enjoyable. I would be delighted to hear your comments on the book, paintings and poems via my website contact page, see www.maggieweirwilson.co.uk. Do get in touch and happy reading.

Painting 1. Cauliflower, by Dr Maggie Weir-Wilson

Chapter 1: *In the Beginning*

Medieval life before enclosure

There are faint echoes of allotments in the early medieval landscape. William the Conqueror, who had a good grasp of administration, imposed a manorial system on the people and landscape of England when he took the kingdom. It was a fairly rigid feudal system with everyone in their place. The King owned all the land which he then distributed to his trusted Norman knights and Barons, such as William de Braose who gained lands in Sussex and the Welsh marches. Sussex was divided into five baronies known as rapes, each stretching from the coast up through the Weald to the Surrey border. William de Braose was given Bramber Rape which included his castle at Bramber and a variety of smaller administrative areas called manors, such as Washington and Beeding, which were further divided into parishes.

There was the King at the top of the feudal hierarchy, then the nobility and the lords of the manors. Under them were the peasantry, in the 11th century about eighty-five per cent of the population. However, the peasantry had its stations. First were the Yeoman who were reasonably independent, having their own areas of land and cottages and few obligations to their lord. A wealthy Yeoman could own an area known as a virgate, twelve hectares or thirty acres, so they could feed their family and also sell their produce. Then came the villeins and cottagers who worked not only on their own strips of land but those of the Lord of the Manor as well. They paid rent for their strips of land in work and produce, which would include animals, and they were obligated to fight for their lord. Amongst this group were also the craftspeople; the blacksmiths, bakers, carpenters, millers and such like who were obligated to work for the lord. There was also a section of society who were slaves, and so considered property of the lord who could be bought and sold, and who were totally reliant on the lord.

The land outside the village, castle or manor house would consist of open fields, no hedges or fences, meadowland, wood pasture and woodland. The lord may have a separate field from the local people on which they would work, but their own patches would be unfenced strips of land, perhaps marked by stones or ridges, and scattered through the open fields. Thus, there had to be community agreement on ploughing, sowing, harvesting and threshing, with everyone pitching in. Not only did the lord take his cut, but the church did too through the tithes expected from everyone. Tithe Barns were built in order to store this taxed produce. One such barn is the Holbrook Tithe Barn, appropriately now a community centre.

The type of crops grown were wheat, barley, oats, peas and beans. People would also keep chickens, pigs and maybe the odd cow or horse. Cottage gardens were used to grow herbs, fruit and other edibles. The diet was basic, bread, beans, peas, eggs and weak beer. Unsurprisingly, foraging on the commons, wasteland and in the forest, plus a bit of poaching, supplemented their meals. However, poaching from royal forests was severely punished under Forest Law. Common meadows were used to produce hay to feed cattle and horses through the winter, as were the commons and woodland. Villagers also used them to graze their few animals. Pigs would root for acorns and beech nuts, known as beechmast, in autumn to fatten for winter. There was a balance of common rights and obligations, but it was a life of relentless hard physical work for both men and women.

Diggers, the earliest allotment activists?

When obligations such as taxes became more onerous, perhaps unsurprisingly, people revolted. One such time was the Civil War, 1642-1651, when the old certainties of religion and monarchy came into question and, in the phrase coined by historian, Christopher Hill, the medieval world turned upside down. Cromwell won, Charles I was executed in 1649, a republic was setup and Christmas was cancelled. New political and religious groups were created by the common people, such as the Seekers, Ranters, Levellers and Diggers.

Out of this turmoil walked the radical Gerrard Winstanley. Born in Wigan in 1609 to a long-established family of traders in cloth, he moved to London when he was twenty to become apprenticed in the cloth business. Here he read, attended his local parish church, married a Susan King, and set up his own business. However, following the Irish rebellion in 1641 and the start of the Civil War, his business collapsed and he and his wife moved to Cobham, Surrey, where they owned land. He began to write and notably called the business of trade *the neat art of thievery and oppressing fellow creatures.*

Cobham was a small rural parish where he was able to keep cows but had to pay the local taxes. Nearby was a large common, part of which was the area of St George's Hill, Weybridge. He became increasingly aware of the inequality and unfairness of the wealthy freeholders who took taxes and overstocked the commons to the detriment of the poor.

By 1648 Winstanley was writing radical texts, and in that year, he was said to have had a powerful visionary trance. Religiously he moved towards the Seekers, rejecting formal church hierarchy and services. He talked not of Christ and scriptures but of a god of true reason, available within every person. Politically he criticised private property, buying and selling; capitalism in other words, saying it induced covetousness, and that the spirit of community would replace it. This was essentially the radical message of the Diggers. At this time there was much optimistic talk of tackling poverty, change and reform, while the Civil War raged. It was hoped that all the commons and wastes would be opened and available to the poor, although even at this early time, enclosure of land for private gain had been happening.

Winstanley finally felt that words were not enough and it was time for action. So, in spring 1649 he took his spade and broke ground on St George's Hill, setting up the first Digger community. He declared that the earth should be set free from the entanglements of priests and landlords and become a common treasury. A manifesto was produced, other Digger communities were set up, and thus it was hoped that both the idea and the action would spread through England and the world. The earth would be returned to its rightful owners, the people. Local communities would share land, growing food so no one went hungry. An equal society invested in their local land and community.

Sadly, there was a violent response to this first community at St George's Hill. Diggers were hit and threatened with mutilation, their tools were broken and a house destroyed. Attempts were made to forcibly evict them and their vegetable patches were flattened. The army was then sent in and the Digger leaders, Winstanley amongst them, were required to account for their activities at Whitehall. They were ridiculed in London pamphlets, and the Cobham locals worried about threats to private property.

1.The Diggers, 1649, image: https://spartacus- educational.com/STUdiggers.htm

The whole Digger experiment had lasted about a year. Diggers drifted away from St George's Hill and from their other colonies in Iver and Wellingborough after vitriolic attacks from the clergy. Although the physical digging of the commons ceased, the ideas of community, equality and non-violence surfaced in the new Quaker movement of the 1650s. Winstanley welcomed Quaker missionaries and died a Quaker in 1676. His legacy lives on and in some circles, he is seen as the earliest activist in the international allotment movement.

The first allotment movement, 1793-1830

Agriculture was changing in the eighteenth century in the way that land was owned and used. Farming was shifting from the feudal open system, with co-operation and the exercise of common rights, to the enclosure of fields for individual landowners and farmers. It is estimated that between 1760 and 1820, thirty per cent of agricultural land in England was enclosed by Acts of Parliament. There were, of course, regional differences particularly in Sussex where the coastal plain was given over to large prosperous farms growing wheat and barley, with the fattening of cattle and sheep on the South Downs. Horsham, on the edge of the High Weald was a marginal land of heath and woodland, more suitable for animal husbandry.

Along with changes in ownership of land came the invention of mechanisation in which larger farms could benefit. In 1701 Jethro Tull invented the seed drill, and a decade later a horse drawn hoe. In 1784, Andrew Meikle invented the threshing machine in which sheaves of corn were fed into a rotating drum which efficiently separated the chaff from the corn, and which could be powered by water, horses, or later, steam. Growing mechanisation of agriculture meant fewer labourers were needed, although the population was growing, almost doubling in the last half of the eighteenth century.

It is perhaps unsurprising that the southern counties of England were most affected by these changes as there was little industry for employment, mostly it was in agriculture. Many found themselves landless, jobless and hungry. More were forced to seek Parish relief and this led to a rise in the rates and much pointless, futile work. Those that were employed saw their wages reduced to below living standards. Added to this desperate situation were the poor harvests at the turn of the century reducing availability and rising prices. However, this did not go unnoticed and the first allotment movement could be said to have begun with the Earl of Winchilsea writing a letter to the Board of Agriculture in 1796 with eight suggestions to alleviate the distress through the provision of land. One of these suggestions was the letting of a small piece of wasteland to a poor labourer. Providing farm cottages with gardens and a cow was another.

Although many opposed these ideas, particularly farmers, enough saw the benefit and in the same year the Society for Bettering the Condition and Increasing the Comforts of the Poor (SBCP) was set up providing welfare for the poor and contributing to the first allotment movement. The first allotments were in Wiltshire and Gloucestershire. The very first was said to be in Great Somerford, Wiltshire, in 1809. Generally, the numbers were limited and set up by only a few philanthropic estate owners, mainly members of the SBCP Committee. However, it was a start and the idea gradually gained momentum.

As the nineteenth century dawned discontent was in the air. The Napoleonic Wars ended in 1815 releasing more men looking for employment. Six years later, William Cobbett, farmer, soldier and political commentator from Surrey went on his Rural Rides, writing up his impressions, writing radical articles and giving stirring speeches, much reported by newspapers. He was shocked by the impact of enclosure on labourers and the rural community. In July 1823 he rode from Worth to Horsham through St Leonard's Forest and onto, 'a large common, now enclosed, cut up, disfigured, spoiled, and the labourer all driven from its skirts. I have seldom travelled over eight miles so well calculated to fill the mind with painful reflections.' Damning assessment indeed.

Horsham Common was an open area of about 689 acres, which wrapped around the town from the north-west to the east. The soil was owned by the Lord of the Manor, the Duke of Norfolk, while fifty-two town burgesses or property owners, had the right to graze animals, gather resources, and also on mutual agreement to lease out small parcels of land. Everyone had a right to walk across the common and many town events were held there, including hangings. In 1812 the Duke of Norfolk took a bill to Parliament for the enclosure of the common and its division into private farms and plots. The wealthy Robert Henry Hurst of Park House bought a considerable amount of common land from the duke.

By 1830 the general population had had enough of poverty and the Swing Riots emerged first in Kent and Sussex. A haystack was torched and burnt in June of that year in Orpington, Kent and there followed an escalation of rick burning and destruction of threshing machines. Threatening notes were left for the owners or farmers who were condemned as, ... *enemies of the people on all occasions.* and signed by a 'Captain Swing'. A Horsham Magistrate, Sir Timothy Shelley received a note that told him to listen to the labourers' complaints or, '… beware the fatal dagger.' which has disturbing echoes of toxic social media messages today.

Fires and destruction were less common in Horsham than in other parts of Sussex, Kent and Surrey. This was not because labourers were any less poverty stricken but because the tradesmen and farmers here showed a certain sympathy with their situation and demands. On several occasions the Magistrates refused to swear in special constables to repress the labourers, however this was not to last.

Late 1830 became known as the Mobbing Winter when large mobs of labourers demanded liveable wages. Horsham did not escape their attentions and on 18th November 1830, a crowd of about 1500 angry labourers turned up at Horsham Magistrates' homes demanding agreement over better wages. One of these was the elderly Sir Timothy Shelley at Field Place, who greeted them generously but they insisted on him coming with them to a Vestry Meeting at Horsham church to demand higher wages and lower tithes. It took time and threats, with Robert Hurst holding out the longest and many convinced violence would be done to him. However, agreement was finally made. The anger of the mob was dissipated, although smaller groups of men went from house-to-house demanding money. Mostly they got it due to some public sympathy, but also it must have been quite frightening. The following day more than thirty special constables were sworn in, and even the military were called in by some Horsham Magistrates, although no lives or property had been lost.

The rioting faded as quickly as it had appeared, mainly due to arrests and harsh punishments, but perhaps also due to the Great Reform Act of 1832 which broadened the voting franchise. Previous to this Act, old parliamentary boroughs like Horsham had the right to send two Members of Parliament to the House of Commons, no matter the size of the population they represented. At this time Horsham's fifty-two burgesses voted by a show of hands in an open meeting, most voted with their wealthy and powerful landowners, Lord and Lady Irwin or the Duke of Norfolk, with or without bribery. Not surprisingly, Horsham was at this time known as one of the worst *rotten boroughs*. However, the 1832 Reform Act gave hope for change and a fairer society.

The second allotment movement, 1832-1914

There is no doubt that the Swing Riots raised the profile of widespread poverty and touched the consciences of the better off. There had been legislation in 1831-2 permitting and encouraging parishes to establish allotments but not much progress had been made, mainly due to opposition by local farmers. However, the desperation of agricultural workers remained dire and in 1834, only a few years after the Swing Riots, a group of Dorset labourers attempted to set up a trade union. They were arrested and sentenced to seven years transportation to Australia with hard labour. Their plight engendered much public support, the group becoming known as the Tolpuddle Martyrs. They were pardoned three years later and returned to a heroes' welcome.

An interesting and influential person in the fight against poverty and injustice through the promotion of allotments was Mrs Mary Ann Gilbert of Eastbourne, the wife of Davies Gilbert, last President of the Board of Agriculture, disbanded 1822. As a landowner she was aware of good agricultural land going out of use, while poor labourers suffered the humiliations of the poor relief with little proper work. She also did not subscribe to the stereotype of the poor being work-shy. She began by experimenting with the enrichment of an area near Beachy Head. She employed the poor to move good soil from marshland and spread it on the thin soil of the beach, and then to cultivate potatoes. This proved very successful, and so the area was walled, gated and rented out at 3 pence a rod, or 40 shillings an acre. It was estimated that 174 paupers supported their families on these *allotments*, however, despite this the vestries, or parish committees, full of elected clergy, landowners and farmers, were hesitant to back her.

Mrs Gilbert was convinced that from her experience the allotment system and its encouragement of good growing practices were the answer to restoring independence and good moral values to the poor of Sussex. She continued to experiment and improve her allotment system, such as supplying tanks to catch rainwater and reducing waste in the sowing and storage of wheat. In 1830 she had about fifty allotment tenants but by 1835 she had 213, mostly all feeding their families and paying rent. To enhance her tenants' knowledge further she set up two self-supporting agricultural schools for their children, wrote papers, and attracted considerable interest from as far away as the United States. She was a true pioneer in establishing the value of allotments in relieving poverty and encouraging independence, learning and dignity amongst the poorer classes.

Another influential person regarding the establishment of allotments was a London surgeon, Benjamin Wills, who raised the radical idea that land should be acquired for the poor, divided into small farms, initially rented free, and that all agricultural cottages should have two acres for the family to cultivate for themselves. Wills formed The Labourers' Friend Society (LFS) in 1830. The society said that a poor labourer spending useful time working his own plot would feel more a part of society, he would have a stake in the British soil and gain respect in his community. Not surprisingly Mrs Gilbert became an early member.

The LFS published monthly magazines which circulated to landowners, clergy and others who might be persuaded to give allotments of land to the local poor. The magazine covered progress in the national allocation of allotments, plus other means of improving the lot of the poor labourer. Examples were the establishment of clothes clubs, loan societies and libraries, plus it ran helpful articles on subjects such as producing eggs, how to make the most of a single cow, the necessity of weeding. Each month it always published an update on Ireland, the Irish potato famine having begun in 1845, and it often gave updates on the West Indies.

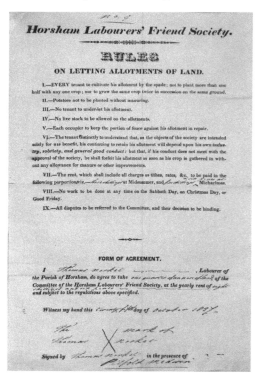

2. Agreement between Horsham Labourers' Friend Society and Thomas Norket for plot No. 9, site unknown. Horsham Museum 2001.499.15.

As the idea and success of allotments grew, more local branches of the LFS were established. Archived in Horsham Museum are handwritten notes of a meeting chaired by Robert Aldridge on 11th April 1837 which resolved to form the Horsham Labourers' Friend Society for the purpose of promoting and encouraging the cutting of allotments of land for the poor. There was to be a request made to the Duke of Norfolk to fill the office of Patron. The new society clearly moved fast as eight days later there was a list of thirty-four local labourers who were to be allocated an allotment plot, although on what site is unclear. Most were men in their thirties and forties with an average of four to six children, although at least one had eight children. From this time is an agreement for a plot nine between Horsham Labourers' Friend Society and a new allotment holder, Thomas Norket, who could not write but put his mark on the agreement. It was witnessed by Pilfold Medwin, who is mentioned later as a trustee.

It is interesting to see what the rules required at that time, not to plant more than half the plot with the same crop, to succession plant and to always manure the potatoes. A plot holder was also required to be industrious, sober and of good conduct, and not to work the plot on Christian holidays such as a Sunday, Christmas Day and Easter Friday.

An audit of the Horsham Labourers' Friend Society in June 1839 showed that it rented three allotment sites; north-west with seventeen plots, south-east with sixteen plots and eastern, also with sixteen plots, with rents paid to the RH Hurst Estate, Mr Bridger and Mr Botting. A year later another site, Star, was added with eight plots. It was not made clear where these sites were but looking at the 1840 Horsham Tithe Map Schedule and Index (with maps redrawn by Alan Siney and published in 1998) it shows that the Horsham Labourers' Friend Society rented a large plot in New Street, owned by Elizabeth Bridger; two small plots on what is now Trafalgar Road, owned by the Duke of Norfolk; and one on the Crawley Road next to the workhouse, owned by Robert Hurst. One could therefore surmise that the north-west allotment site, with a mention of the Dog and Bacon public house, was the one along Trafalgar Road, the one on the Crawley Road was the Star, near the public house of that name. The New Street site was perhaps the Eastern site, near where Clarence Road allotments were in later years.

Annual shows were very much a feature of the Horsham Labourers' Friend

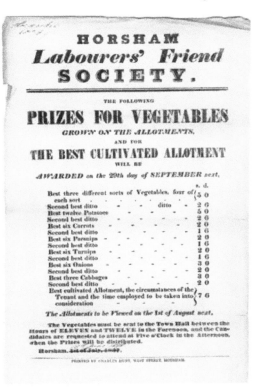

3. Poster from Horsham Labourers Friend Society Advertising Prizes for Vegetables and Best Cultivated Allotment, 1838. Horsham Museum 1998.1667.

Society from the start, with vegetables on show in September at the town hall or the Richmond hotel. A poster from 1838 shows cash prizes paid for best vegetables and the best cultivated allotment which took into consideration the amount of paid employment a plot holder was required to do.

It is clear that the Labourers' Friend Society was dominant in the early establishment of allotments, and although Parliament took an interest and passed clauses promoting them in 1819, 1831 and 1832, it did not have a significant impact. Perhaps this was because the LFS was able to persuade landowners to provide allotments, but farmers tended to be opposed, seeing them as a challenge to a cheap supply of labour.

In 1843 a Select Committee on the Labouring Poor was set up which recommended legislation to ensure plots be a quarter of an acre and close to the houses of the poor, rents would be the usual for farmland and taxes would be paid by the landowner. What followed was the 1845 General Enclosure Act which ensured that any future enclosure of waste land would include allotments for the poor. Sadly, too late for Horsham whose common land was enclosed in 1812-13. However, the concept and fact of allotments were now well established although still rather dependant on landowners leasing land for that purpose. Certainly few allotments were lost in the 19th century, and those that were lost were due to the land being needed for alternative uses rather than lack of demand. The actual sites noted in the Horsham 1840 Tithe Map did not all survive but alternative, perhaps better, sites and more of them were to follow.

In 1882 the Allotment Extension Act was brought into law in order to try and ensure allotments were provided by the Poor Law Commission and charities, but more comprehensive law was needed. Thus in 1887 a new Allotment Act was passed which required Local Authorities to provide allotments if six local voters had requested them and where there was no existing provision. This was followed up in 1908 by the Small Holding and Allotment Act which consolidated previous Acts and created the statutory allotments on which today's laws regarding allotment security for plot holders, and site provision, are based. It gave local authorities the power to compulsorily purchase land for allotments, but also to sell allotment sites if it deemed they were no longer needed. By 1913, two thirds of parishes in England had allotments, with most in the south.

It should be mentioned that an increasing number of middle class urban, and suburban, residents were interested not in allotments as such but in leisure gardens. These were often slightly bigger than a standard allotment of ten poles, were hedged or fenced with lawns, flowers and perhaps had a summer house. Rentals for these small private detached gardens was often a guinea, giving them the name of *Guinea Gardens*. A few, like ones in Warwick, have been kept and restored, and certainly the concept was popular in Europe, but most in Britain have been converted to allotments or built over as the 20th century took hold.

It is perhaps relevant to note at this point that by tradition, allotment plots are measured in rods. This is a unit of measurement from Anglo-Saxon times and supposedly based on the length of a team of oxen and plough. The unit of a pole is interchangeable with a rod as they are the same unit measurement. The normal size of an allotment plot was ten rods/poles which is equivalent to 5.5 square yards or 4.6 square metres. This was regarded as a sufficient size to feed a family of four. These days the plots are often half this size, or less, due to the many other demands of modern life. People seem fond of these ancient measurements and councils are not obliged by any government act to change them to metric and they do not fall within the Units of Measurements Regulations 1994.

Allotment

Ten rods, ten times plough tail to oxen nose
this special strip of soil, ramshackle and random,
cultivated or abandoned.

I weed like weeding women before me
down on my knees in the earth, hands and nails
muddied in soil, timeless tasks.

The soil feels friable like cake crumbs,
I gently ease out each weed by root,
a net of fibres, or tunnelled tap root.

A spider scuttles away, while a small
sandy coloured lizard cowers in the earth,
ants, now agitated, swarm over my feet.

The bees are on a mission, the butterflies
in love, plodding pigeons eye peas in the pod,
red kites circle, watching, above it all.

I remember the casualties from enclosure,
cultivating strips and feeding their families,
ten rods, ten times plough tail to oxen nose.

Chapter 2: *The War Years*

The war years, 1914-1945

From the 1840s, the establishment of free trade increased the import of cheap food such as wheat and sugar from the Americas, so that by the time the First World War broke out, Britain was importing about a third of its food. However, this was to be threatened by war time German U-boats targeting merchant shipping and causing food blockades. Shortages were further aggravated by poor harvests in 1916 and of course the recruitment and requisition of agricultural workers, and horses, for the army. Suddenly, it became an issue of patriotic survival for citizens to grow their own food.

Numbers of allotments increased as the government's Cultivation of Lands Order, 1917 was introduced to secure the cultivation of unoccupied land in districts where labour for cultivation was available through local authorities taking possession of such land. An allotment committee was set up in Horsham Urban District Council made up of four members, Messrs Rowland, Potter, Wheeler and Roberts, in order to encourage and oversee this directive. One of their first requisitions in March 1917 was a small piece of land 3/5ths acre lying south of Depot Road. There was space for ten allotments, two plots side by side stretching down to a pond. It was made clear certain regulations should be observed by the tenants and the owner, Mr Herbert Agate would be compensated at the end of the war for any deterioration of his land.

Allotmentitis gripped the country, the charitable Vacant Land Cultivation Society (VLCS) was pulled in to help and their membership rocketed. *Digging for Dora* became a catchphrase on posters and in newspapers – DORA stood for the Defence of the Realm Act. Role models included King George V who had vegetable plots established at Windsor Castle, Buckingham Palace and around the Albert Memorial in London. Lloyd George, the Prime Minister was said to grow potatoes at his home in Surrey. The Church let it be known that it approved of working on one's allotment on a Sunday and railway companies allowed their spare land to be used for allotments. Even women were encouraged to get involved in growing food. A circular from the government was sent in January 1917, noting that, '… it is essential for the success of the scheme to secure the active co-operation of women in order that female labour should be utilised as fully as possible.'. The Women's Land Army was also set up in 1917.

29

Despite all this effort, Britain was hungry and rationing was brought in during 1918, the war ending in the November of that year. Allotments had definitely helped in feeding the nation and their popularity remained after the war as debt and depression followed. However, those areas of land requisitioned by the government had to be returned to their owners by the end of March 1923, so the numbers of allotments fell. Many of the large original plots of ten poles (which is the same as ten rods, or 250 square metres) were divided to satisfy demand. A number of councils, including Horsham, were prepared to enter into negotiations with owners for the lease of these lands for the purpose of continuing the allotments. Security of tenure had been a problem for allotment holders, councils tending to reclaim allotment sites for alternative purposes such as building, a problem which persists today.

The 1922 Allotment Act went some way to dealing with both the provision and security of tenure of allotments. It also clarified the size and purpose of allotments which has persisted down the years. The plots must not be larger than 40 poles (1,000 square metres) and used only for growing fruit and vegetables by the occupier to feed himself and his family. This meant no selling of produce and no growing of flowers. As far as security of tenure went, any council wanting to sell its allotment land had to obtain government approval first, and also had to give tenants six months' notice. According to a newspaper cutting dated August 12th, 1922, Sir Kingsley Wood, MP for Woolwich West, chair of the Parliamentary Allotments Committee said, 'The Allotment Act, which has just received the Royal Assent, is the allotment holders Magna Carta.' so pleased was he with the increased security of tenure. However, this security of tenure was strengthened further by the 1925 Allotment Act, section 8, which stated that land specifically bought by local councils for allotments could not be sold, or used for any other purpose, without consent from the Ministry of Agriculture. These allotments were now statutory allotments.

The value of allotments in contributing to feeding the hungry came into its own again during the Miners' Strike of 1926 and subsequent General Strike. The strikers were in such a piteous state that the Quakers, or Society of Friends, combined with workers unions to provide food, clothes and the work of repair. By the time of the Wall Street Crash in 1929, Quakers were focussed on providing allotments for the poor in mining areas and by 1933 they had assisted 100,000 unemployed to take on allotments, which was just as well given that another World War would start before the decade was out. Around this time a circular was received by Horsham Urban Council from the Quakers' Friends Allotment Committee asking for the provision of more allotments. Their 1933-34 annual report gave a description of group holdings in Christchurch, Eynsham and Swindon. In these places, groups of twelve men were each provided with a moveable pig shelter and run, four 8-week-old pigs and a balanced ration of food with which to feed them. So, the allotments were not just providing vegetables but animals for meat as well.

There is some indication that pigs were also kept on our Horsham allotments. It was noted that in September 1935, the Sanitary Inspector to the Clerk of Horsham Urban District Council went to inspect some pigsties belonging to an allotment holder situated between Oakhill Road and the Brighton Road, probably Clarence Road allotments today. They were said to be in a very unsatisfactory condition, so the allotment holder was told to repair and clean them. Again, in 1935 a report about allotment sites in Horsham Urban District, recorded that out of the 159 individual allotments held by the council, one was let for pigsties, two for chickens, two were rough and under trees and six were vacant. There were at this time many more allotments let to associations, 623 on forty-nine acres, and there were some let by private owners whose history is more difficult to trace.

In July 1936, the Friends Allotments Committee sent a letter to all councils saying it was desirable to purchase land so that allotments could be permanently secured for growing food and to satisfy such demand. Horsham council did actually reply saying that if necessary, they would buy land. The letter pointed out they had done so in the past. The following year, March 1937, the council received a letter from the Sussex Area of Federated Allotment and Horticultural Societies suggesting that allotments should be brought up to amenity standard by being inspected and marks awarded for merit. This somewhat anticipated the much later Horsham in Bloom awards. However, they received a rather dusty reply from the clerk saying

4. Annual Report from the Friends Allotment Committee 1933-34. WSRO UD/HO/21/2/75.

that the matter hardly came within the jurisdiction of the council as large areas of allotment are not owned by the HUDC, so that was the end of that.

In 1930 the National Allotment Society, later the National Allotment and Gardens Society, was established from combining a number of smaller organisations and unions. Following the Thorpe Report (1969), it added leisure gardens to its title, so that in its final reincarnation it became the National Society of Allotment and Leisure Gardens (NSALG). Since its inception it has worked hard to promote allotments and provide its members with information, legal advice, insurance, discounted seeds and a free quarterly magazine, and still does so today. In 2000, it set up the National Allotment Garden Trust (NAGT) to encourage and educate people on the benefits of allotment growing.

The total numbers of UK allotments fell between the world wars by about half a million to 815,000. Thus, Britain was in no way self-sufficient in food by the outbreak of the Second World War in September 1939. As at the start of the First World War, it was still importing about a third of its food and most of its wheat. Despite advice from nutritional scientists for a national food policy, the government seemed unconcerned and disorganised with regard to addressing likely food shortages.

Food rationing was introduced in 1940, and continued until formally ended in 1954, fourteen years of deprivation and surprisingly healthy eating. Not until the start of the war did the government introduce the Cultivation of Land (Allotments) Order 1939, which allowed local councils to requisition vacant land, parks and fields to turn them into allotments. The message to the people from the Ministry of Agriculture was a rather stark, *Grow More Food*, which was later changed to the somewhat catchier *Dig for Victory* and *The Spade is as Mighty as the Sword.* This new message was backed up by efforts to educate people on how to grow vegetables and cook them, through events, pamphlets, plans, information sheets and books. The Royal Horticultural Society (RHS) pitched in by publishing its hugely successful *The Vegetable Garden Displayed* (1941) and followed in 1951 by *The Fruit Garden Displayed*, both popular.

Women were again encouraged to get into vegetable growing through the revival of the Women's Land Army and through lots of illustrations showing women digging and sowing. New gardening personalities such as Cecil Middleton took to the radio and newspapers with guidance on growing. He also produced a very popular book, *Digging for Victory: Wartime Gardening with Mr Middleton*

(1942). As manure was in short supply, a new inorganic fertiliser called, National Growmore Fertiliser was manufactured and promoted by the government. Growmore is still popular and on sale today.

5. World War II poster promoting the Dig for Victory message.

6. World War II poster encouraging women to grow vegetables.

Generally, the public responded well to the Dig for Victory call to arms and every spare inch of garden, park and allotment were turned to producing fresh vegetables for the family and neighbours. However, this enthusiasm was not to outlast the war effort.

Painting 2. Loganberries, by Dr Maggie Weir-Wilson

Chapter 3: *Modern Times*

Allotment holding went into decline again after the second world war, not helped by the bitterly cold winter of 1947 which froze vegetables in the soil where they grew. By then much of the requisitioned land for allotments had been returned to its owners, thus losing about half a million plots. Security of tenure for allotment holders was improved by a new Allotment Act in 1950, so that notices to quit were increased from six months to a year. This act also abolished restrictions on the keeping of hens and rabbits. But this did not halt the decline. Caroline Foley notes in her book, *Of Cabbages and Kings: The History of Allotments* that in the 1960s the number of plots nationwide was down to 729,000, ten years later it was 532,000, and it was suggested that one out of five plots were neglected. The caricature of allotments and allotment holders at this time was of ramshackle sheds, poverty and old men in flat caps and braces growing cabbages. Shifts in lifestyle undoubtedly played a part in the decline, such as the easy availability of frozen food and pre-prepared meals from supermarkets, an increase in women working, long work hours and commuting.

In the 1960s, the government did show some concern about the decline in allotment provision and use, so a committee was set up which produced the Thorpe Report in 1969. It recommended a total overhaul of allotment law and suggested more leisure gardens be provided. Harry Thorpe went as far as redesigning several allotment sites to incorporate leisure gardens with lawns and flowers to attract the middle classes, but this was not as popular as it was in Europe. True to form his recommendations were all ignored by the government. However, the report did usefully recommend that fifteen ten-pole plots should be provided per thousand households, and this remains a rule of thumb for local councils today, although the actual plots are mostly split into smaller and more manageable sizes.

Allotment numbers continued to decline with the suspicion that councils were happy to see them go as they could then sell the land to developers. However, perhaps more at risk was the private land owned by, for example, the railway companies and the Church who were happy to sell off now redundant land. Pete Riley in his book, *Economic Growth: Allotments Campaign Guide* suggests that from 1969-79 approximately 8,000 plots were lost from railway land and 40,000 from private land. So that by the 1980s there were only about 300,000 plots left in the UK. However, an interesting development was the launch of the Federation of City Farms and Community Gardens at the House of Lords in 1988. This was a response to the number of disused and derelict sites in cities and town centres, with an eye to creating stronger communities and improving the environment.

In 1998 a further governmental investigation, the House of Commons inquiry into the Future for Allotments, was set up to look into the decline of traditional allotments. They noted that the provision of allotments was at its lowest level since the 1887 Allotments Act. However, the committee also noted that allotments were, in fact, important in the cultural landscape as well as for general health and wellbeing, particularly for the older generation. Again, they recommended an overhaul of allotment law and the modernisation of local authority rules on what could, or could not, be found on plots and allotment sites generally. They noted that replacement plots were not always provided when old ones were lost, and recommendations to address this were made. Yet again, no new legislation was passed. However, growing your own food had become slightly more fashionable and desirable thanks to programmes on the TV in the mid-1970s like *The Good Life*. Thankfully, there were moves in various other quarters which began a renewed interest and enthusiasm for allotments. In 2000 the magazine, *Amateur Gardening* began a campaign for more allotments which involved NSALG, and various celebrities, so raising the profile of allotments. In 2001 the government published a guide to best practice called *Growing in the Community* which encouraged councils to promote allotments.

Initially, in the mid-1970s, the environmental pressure group Friends of the Earth began a campaign for the provision of more allotments on pieces of waste land in urban areas. In 1979 they produced *Economic Growth: Allotments Campaign Guide* by Pete Riley, a guide for activists from local communities in lobbying for more allotments by engaging their local councils. Local groups from Friends of the Earth were particularly successful in Lambeth, Tyneside, Redbridge and Oxford. Another campaign was the charitable Allotment Regeneration Initiative (ARI) which was set up to revive interest in allotments. It helped to put the government's *Growing in the Community* into practice and it published its own guide in 2007. It also ran valuable training for local authority officers before it came to an end in 2012 and its work was taken on by NSALG.

By the new millennium environmental and sustainability concerns had gained some traction following books like *Silent Spring*, by Rachel Carson, published in 1962, which set alarm bells ringing over the use of DDT and the move in America to industrial style farming based on economic considerations only. When James Rebanks, farmer in Cumbria, read *Silent Spring*, it started him on a journey to gradually change his farm practices from the sole aim of economic profit to that of caring for nature and bringing back all the species that had been lost by the overuse of chemical pesticides and fertilisers. In his recent book *English Pastoral An Inheritance*, he says:

'… a significant share of our nutrition should be produced locally so we can see it, participate in it, and question and challenge it when we need to. Food production is too important to be pushed out of sight and out of mind. Foodstuffs from anonymous distant global sources are rarely subject to our rules and regulations on welfare, environment or hygiene or produced in line with our values.' From *English Pastoral An Inheritance*, by James Rebanks (2020) p.264.

Ahead if its time with these same concerns were farmers and scientists in the late 1940s who set up the Soil Association, a charity which now certifies organic and sustainable schemes. Another charity, Garden Organic, formerly known as, Henry Doubleday Research Association, offers the Heritage Seed Library and lots of growing advice as well as encouraging local associations, such as Horsham Organic Gardeners which organises regular speakers and garden trips in the summer. Concern for the continuing loss of pollinators through the use of pesticides, absence of weeds and hedgerows, and the over tidying of gardens led Dave Goulson, Professor of Biological Sciences at the University of Sussex, to produce his book *The Garden Jungle: or Gardening to Save the Planet* in 2019. This gives an insight into the lives of unappreciated creatures in our gardens and allotments, what they do for us and the planet, and why we should understand and respect them, rather than unthinkingly destroy them. He has recently followed this up with his 2021 book *Silent Earth: Averting the Insect Apocalypse*, which is an even stronger call for understanding and tolerance.

On a similar theme, and local to Horsham, is the Knepp Estate, where, in a brave and unprecedented move early in the millennium, owners Charlie Burrell and Isabella Tree began to switch from unproductive intensive farming on unpromising clay soil to just allowing nature to take over. This they called *rewilding* and it required minimum human intervention plus free ranging cattle, pigs and ponies. Despite lots of criticism at the time in the letters page of the local paper, twenty-two years later the Knepp Estate is a terrific success in showing how species can be encouraged back with the right environment. White storks, nightingales, purple emperor butterflies and turtle doves have all returned, and the enterprise has the wholehearted support of Sir David Attenborough, with the idea is being replicated elsewhere. Isabella Tree writes about their story in her book *Wilding: The Return of Nature to a British Farm*, originally published in 2018, and a fascinating read.

With continuing worries over climate change came the first Earth Summit at Rio de Janeiro in 1992. Allotments were no longer seen as just land to provide cheap food for poor families, but to provide a more ecological solution to a number of concerns; such as, being active in saving food miles by avoiding out of season vegetables and fruit, growing good quality food without pesticides and herbicides or genetic modification, improving the soil quality, avoiding plastic packaging and developing good health, wellbeing and community.

In the decades since, allotments have continued to grow in popularity and desirability. In 2006 the Transition Towns movement came into being, which encouraged growing your own. Indeed, Transition Horsham (http://www.transitionhorsham.org.uk/) set up a Community Allotment at the Chesworth site in about 2011, which is still going strong as can be seen in Chapter 7 regarding Chesworth Allotment site. Another movement based on similar concerns over climate change and future wellbeing was Incredible Edible Todmorden. This was where a former Yorkshire mill town started turning every spare bit of public land, grass verges, roundabouts, into growing fruit and vegetables. Run by volunteers and free for anyone to harvest. Established by two women, Estelle Brown and Mary Clear, about fifteen years ago, it now has about seventy growing sites in the town and is a community benefit society.

In other developments, NSALG set up a National Allotment Week in August every year which includes competitions. Likewise, the Royal Horticultural Society (RHS) now encourages allotment gardens in their annual shows. With the development of their new world food garden and world food café in 2021 they have managed to showcase the growing of many exotic, as well as traditional, vegetables. There has been an increasing interest in unusual vegetables due in part to the diversity of new plot holders. This was very well illustrated by the 2007 film *Grow your Own*. It told the story of the challenges to the old allotmenteers by new migrants taking on a plot and growing seed from their homeland, a type of melon, which helped them heal their grief through leaving. Also, it showed the threats to allotment sites by new developments, in this case a telephone mast, and the joy of the community pulling together to protect their allotments and the new friends made on those allotments.

Today there are lots more *how to* books on growing, as well as jokey tales about allotmenteering such as *Minding my Peas and Cucumbers: Quirky Tales of Allotment Life* by Kay Sexton and the more recent memoir by Tony Walton *My Life on a Hillside Allotment* about growing up in the Rhondda Valley and gardening on an allotment for fifty years, man and boy. Tony is now a media star being regularly on the Radio 4 Jeremy Vine show with his tips and hints. Also, now popular are websites such as John Harrison's Allotment & Gardens (www.allotment-garden. org) which gives tips and guidance, a monthly newsletter and discounts for seeds and equipment. On Facebook there is UK Allotments and Allotment Junkies, to mention just two, which are communities that encourage new growers and give lots of advice. Of course, individual allotment sites including five of our local Horsham ones have private Facebook groups for their plot holders which inform and alert, plus they offer surplus produce and plants.

The increasing concern for the environment, sustainability and loss of species, particularly pollinators, have led to a better appreciation of the importance of leaving some weeds, like dandelions and buttercups, for the bees. Building bee hotels for solitary bees and other insects has also gained popularity, being less tidy and leaving those logs and leaves for other residents of allotments such as hedgehogs and beetles. Some of the larger Horsham allotment sites like Chesworth, Roffey and Bennetts Road now have wildlife plots, as can be seen in the following chapters. Most allotments now grow flowers for cutting, which not only attracts pollinators but saves on imports, airmiles and plastic wrapping.

After the warm, dry summer of 2022 something to also consider for the future – which ties in with diversity and sustainability – is the ability to continue to water plots when water companies are restricting use. It is suggested that one year in every four or five will be really dry. It seems sensible then that in addition to mains water, allotment sites give serious consideration to water harvesting systems and storage which can then be used in drought conditions. Of course, the better health of the soil, the better it can cope with drought, so techniques such as heavy mulching and the no dig technique improves the structure and resilience of the soil.

An interesting recent move regarding the provision of allotment sites has been from housing developers, some of whom are now putting allotment sites within their plans. For example, when Linden Homes were marketing the Graylingwell Park development in Chichester in 2011 they promised allotments and an orchard on site for the new home buyers, to be managed by Chichester Community Development Trust. Sadly, eleven years on Linden Homes have gone and Drew Smith now own the development with no sign of any allotments, but if they do come they will be council run and open to all. Another development closer to home, is Highwood Village being built by Berkeley Group on the western edge of Horsham and due to be completed in 2025. It has an allotment site marked out in its plans by the River Arun on the south-eastern edge of the development. In autumn 2022 the site was marked out in plots in a dogleg shape and covered in black plastic. Initial enquiries will be to the council although I suspect they will encourage management by a new society.

7. Model in the Highwood Village Sales Office showing the allotment site.

8. Actual site of allotments marked out in black plastic.

This section on the increasing popularity and demand for allotments should rightly end with the Covid pandemic of 2020-22. Under lockdown rules when people were allowed out for an hour's exercise, without socialising, allotments were the perfect solution, particularly for those without gardens. Whilst getting exercise and fresh air, one could shout across to friends on neighbouring plots and tend to one's all-important fruit and vegetables while providing the family with lots of good organic local produce. No wonder the demand for allotments has increased everywhere and there are long waiting lists on each of the Horsham town sites. Which leads us nicely on to the following chapters about each individual Horsham town allotment site.

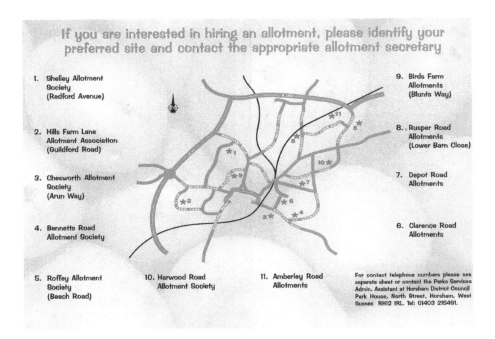

If you are interested in hiring an allotment, please identify your preferred site and contact the appropriate allotment secretary

1. Shelley Allotment Society (Redford Avenue)

2. Hills Farm Lane Allotment Association (Guildford Road)

3. Chesworth Allotment Society (Arun Way)

4. Bennetts Road Allotment Society

5. Roffey Allotment Society (Beech Road)

10. Harwood Road Allotment Society

11. Amberley Road Allotments

9. Birds Farm Allotments (Blunts Way)

8. Rusper Road Allotments (Lower Barn Close)

7. Depot Road Allotments

6. Clarence Road Allotments

For contact telephone numbers please see separate sheet or contact the Parks Services Admin. Assistant at Horsham District Council Park House, North Street, Horsham, West Sussex RH12 1RL. Tel: 01403 215491.

9. From HDC leaflet (circa 2010) Grow your Own! Allotments in Horsham. Showing position of all eleven allotment sites in central Horsham. No. 2 Hills Farm Lane no longer available. With kind permission of Horsham District Council.

Fox

I'm sitting on my bucket

enjoying the break

and a banana

when a fox walks by

keeping to the grass paths

investigating

Sunny October

early afternoon

people are busy

but I see him

our local grape thief

casing the allotment.

Chapter 4: *Amberley Close Allotments*

10. Entrance to Amberley Close Allotments from Amberley Close.

Amberley Close Allotments are one of the few sites still managed by North Horsham Parish Council and not by its own independent allotment association. It is a small site of thirty plots, some full and most half sized, tucked away between the end of Amberley Close and the railway line. Annual charges in 2020 were £30 for a full plot and £15 for half, reviewed yearly.

Remembering the past

North Horsham Parish Council Clerk informed me that they had a land certificate confirmation of the transfer of land from Federated Design and Building Group Limited to Horsham Rural Parish Council dated 14th May 1969. This is in line with what Seton Wood remembers of the establishment of the allotments.

Seton and Bryony Wood have been Amberley Close Allotment holders since the allotment site was established. They explained to me that Federated Homes had built the estate around Amberley Road in the 1960s, about four hundred houses in all. They had set aside land for the North Horsham By-Pass, the A264, with

43

three different options. Once the path of the by-pass had been settled, some of this spare land was designated as open public space. It seems there had always been a footpath and bridle way from this open space to Owls Castle Farm, which now crossed the railway line and the by-pass. When Federated Homes went bankrupt Horsham Rural Parish Council took over the public space, most of it was to be for recreation and the small triangular corner for allotments. A Hawthorn hedge was planted dividing the two uses. That hedge, which Seton Wood remembers being planted in muddy holes in a rain-soaked field, is now nine-foot-high and eight-foot-wide and needs to be cut every year.

11. Seton Wood on the Amberley Allotments site. Photo with kind permission of Jim Penberthy.

Remembering how these allotments got started, Seton explained how in the early 1970s, he and a group of keen allotmenteers got together on a Saturday and using his 50m tape measure and small posts pegged out twenty plots. The plots were about 11m x 8m which, although big, were smaller than the national average in order to get them all into the odd triangular shape of the site. As noted, many are now split in two in order to be easier to manage for working people. Also more women are working the plots. Plots sixteen, twenty and seventeen were also different sizes due to the large oak trees on the boundary.

12. Large hawthorn hedge dividing the allotment site from recreational space.

There is obviously not much room for sheds, and so permission has to be granted from North Horsham Parish Council. The shed on plot thirteen had to be moved from one side of the plot to the other to prevent shading on the adjacent plot. Plots eighteen and nineteen were not originally part of the plan as it was thought that lorries delivering manure would need space to turn around but this did not prove to be the case and so plots eighteen and nineteen were able to be added to Seton's original plot plan.

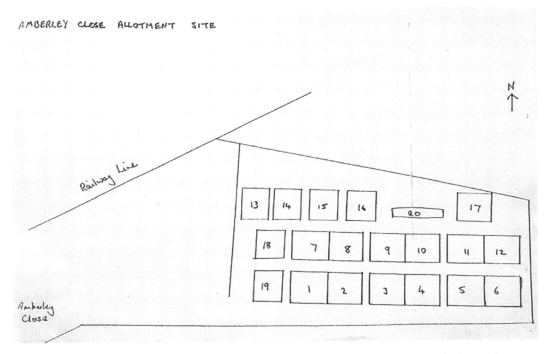

13. Seton Wood's plan of the allotment plots at Amberley Close. With kind permission of Seton Wood.

Water pipes have been a bit of a problem over the years. There are currently two standpipes and one tank and the pipes supplying these originally ran down the middle of the grassy access path. Seton was however, able to move this to one side so that the occasional car or lorry could pass without damaging the pipes. However, when more houses were being built around the allotment site, their water mains were driven right through the row of allotment plots nineteen and one to six, much to these allotment holders' dismay and annoyance. Seton can remember when the outlook from the plots were not houses but farms, fields and cattle, with the odd rogue chicken coming to visit.

Allotment stories

14. Judy Clark on her allotment. Photo with kind permission of Judy Clark.

Allotment holder Judy Clark told me the following story, reproduced in her own words with a slight bit of editing from me:

'It was a perfect scorching August Bank Holiday Monday when we set off for the allotment with a battered garden tool bag, sunglasses and hats, promising to sort out the tangled muddle before the onset of Autumn. Grateful for long trousers and wellington boots, we traipsed through high stinging nettles. Smelling the earthy dampness in the humid air, we pushed open the ill-fitting wooden gate to the familiar variety of plots. Waving at our neighbours who had the same idea, we enjoyed the warmth and set to work.

'In the distance we heard the routine sound of the train on the track running alongside the allotment. The peace was sharply interrupted as we heard an ear-splitting sound of metal tangled on metal reverberating across the silence. I looked up to see Dave, my husband, running towards the railway line. I dropped my secateurs and followed, quickening my pace as we heard the train come to a halt. Expecting to find the metal tube on its side, we were puzzled that it was in one piece.

'Dog walkers began to gather and murmur as we watched the bewildered passengers on the train. Fingers were pressed on phones calling the emergency services and voices became shouts with shocked faces showing distress. For those who were recently arrived on the scene, people seemed disorientated, what to do, where to go, what to say. A Network Rail van arrived and we hoped it was *leaves on the line* or a technical fault. We headed back to the allotment as the emergency services arrived and there was no more we could do.'

From later reports of this incident, it appeared that on this warm Bank

Holiday Monday, 2020, a woman in her fifties had been hit by a train and died at the scene. Judy later picked a bunch of sweet peas and laid them near the track.

A story from another allotment holder, Jim Penberthy – who has a rather wonderful and prolific fig tree on his allotment – was that about fifteen years ago there had been an awful plague of blackflies that covered everything. The blackfly had appeared mid-week and allotment holders tried everything to get rid of them. Then on the Saturday they were suddenly all gone. There was a rumour that a tourist airplane, probably from nearby Gatwick, had flown over and dropped a load of aviation fuel onto the allotment and killed all the blackfly.

15. Jim Penberthy in front of the fig tree on his allotment. Photo with kind permission of Jim Penberthy.

16. Home-made bug hotel.

Amberley Close allotment site today

The allotment site is not secured behind fencing and gates but is well overlooked by houses and so gets very little trouble. Some years ago, they did get empty bottles thrown over the hedge from the recreational space but this is no longer a problem. There are no designated wildlife spaces as the whole site is too small, but one allotment holder has made a rather nice large bug house on their own allotment.

A very recent problem, thinking about wildlife, is not only foxes but now deer have found the allotment site. This may well be due to the considerable new housing developments in North Horsham driving the deer to look for alternative food supplies and they have found a good one with the allotments.

There are allotment rules that every tenant must agree to. A rather good one is that plot holders are not allowed to sleep overnight on their allotments, presumably it is fine to have a couple of winks during the day! More usual rules are that herb, flower, fruit and vegetable crops are for personal use only, trees must not exceed a height of two metres, no bonfires on site, no sprinklers or hosepipes can be used, no livestock, and sheds or greenhouses only with permission. On two sides there are boundaries of oak trees and brambles which can impinge on the allotments near them, but paths must be kept neat and hedges trimmed.

Generally, the site is well kept and tended, and due to the rules, there are very few structures like sheds or toilets to take away from the impression of serious vegetable and fruit growing. At the time of writing, there was of course a waiting list.

Painting 3. Rhubarb, by Dr Maggie Weir-Wilson

Chapter 5: *Bennetts Road Allotments*

17. General views of Bennetts Road Allotment site.

The allotment site is about two acres (0.8 ha) with fifty plot holders. It is situated next to Bennetts Road playing field, off the Brighton Road, and adjacent to the Scout hut. Within the Scout hut, and immediately noticeable, is the Montessori Nursery School which rents a small allotment plot for its pupils. The Bennetts Road Allotment Association have managed the allotment site since taking over from Horsham District Council management in 1986, probably one of the first sites in Horsham to do so. The committee for the association meets regularly to manage the site. Like most allotment sites in Horsham the land is still owned by HDC and leased to the association, the lease being renewed every ten years, the next renewal in 2027, with rents fixed for five years.

Documentation from Horsham District Council held by the secretary of the committee, Janet Priestley, confirms that the allotment site was established as a statutory site in November 1947 when 2.927 acres were taken to create allotments from housing development land. Further evidence of the age of the site is from John Commins of Harwood Road allotments who has an agreement stating that his father rented plot fifteen (ten rods) on Bennetts Farm allotments in 1955 from Horsham Urban District Council. The yearly rent at this time was 8s 4d paid on 1st

18. General views of Bennetts Road Allotment site.

19. Communal greenhouses and compost toilet.

April. The rules were to cultivate in the proper manner as an allotment garden only, no fruit bushes or trees, not to sublet, and notice to be a full year.

The association pays for water, the maintenance of boundary hedges and insurance. There are three water taps with keys to access the taps. Permission from the committee has to be sought for the erection of any structures like sheds, greenhouses and polytunnels so few, apart from small old ones, are evident. There are three greenhouses that can be communally shared and people tend to have boxes for tools and essentials. One of the greenhouses is in the community area near the school and the other two are up near the wildlife plot. Up here is also a composting toilet, fully accessible for people with reduced mobility and wheelchair users, which was obtained through Big Lottery Funding of £10,000 in 2015. It was the first allotment association in West Sussex to obtain such an award. The toilet was ceremoniously opened on 18th April 2015 by Roy Hughes, a founder member of the Bennetts Road Allotment Association, a trustee and a committee member, who sadly passed away the same year. He had been the longest standing member at the time of the ceremony.

20.Community area with benches and greenhouse.

There are two wildlife plots, at the top and bottom of the site, complete with small ponds and bug house. There is also a rather nice community area with two table benches and the sharing greenhouse.

Remembering the past

Peter Heneghan told me in a Facebook posting that he had, '... so many great memories and stories from the adventures in our allotment, which backed on to our garden in Bennetts Road, even gang warfare over the competition to build the biggest bonfire on fireworks night each year with the boys who lived in Hornbeam Close ... We held out even when the groundworkers came in to develop the allotments into what is now Laurel Walk.'

The Montessori Nursery School

Jacky Brown, Manager of the Montessori Nursery School, which is situated on the boundary of the Bennetts Road Allotments said that she could not emphasise enough the importance of the allotments to the nursery. She explained that Montessori has the ethos of wanting the children to be confident, and have respect for themselves, others and the environment. Children of preschool age, two to five years, have a natural curiosity and want to learn about nature. The Montessori approach encourages the full use of the senses to learn, so smell and texture are paramount.

21. Horsham Montessori Nursery School children enjoying the allotment site. Photo with kind permission of the school - see gallery at www.montessori-uk.co.uk

Jacky explained that the children have their own plot which they can interact with and visit, 'However, the bigger picture is having the children look at the vast variety of colour, texture, smell, and visual experience as they walk around other plot holders' sites. Children see the plants on a timeline from being a small seed and growing to a tall sunflower with large leaves. They experience weight by holding a cabbage and a sprout. They are immersed in all aspects of the Early Years Foundation Stage Statutory Framework. The majority of beautiful blooms are actually their height. It is wonderful to see their faces as they walk past a wall of sweet peas and get excited at the size of a rhubarb leaf.

'They have seen the life cycle of ants, frogs, dragonflies, butterflies, worms in the compost bin, snails and slugs, ladybirds, woodlice, a large fox and many birds ... all at first hand and free in their natural habitat. They hear crickets, birds, lawn mowers, drills, clippers etc.

'They learn to talk to people they do not know. Those children for whom English is not their first language have pleasure in walking around with the teacher and can relax for a little while fulfilling their senses without the need to listen to language. The teachers invite the children, and the children also request, to be taken for a walk. This is an important time when teachers can give 100 per cent attention to the one child. It is all about listening, talking, and being listened to, as well as knowledge building.'

22. Horsham Montessori Nursery School children enjoying the allotment site. Photo with kind permission of the school - see gallery at www.montessori-uk.co.uk

Thinking about the allotment plot itself, Jacky could not actually remember how long the school have had the plot but between five to ten years. She admits that it does not look the prettiest but the children get involved and grow some fruit, herbs, beans, peas, and flowers for wildlife. The school allotment is used not only by themselves. Prior to Covid, they used to have the Horsham QEII School reception class visit and share the gardens, and for those not in wheelchairs, the allotment. It was a lovely reunion once a week. On occasions, again prior to Covid, they had visitors from the local care home come for afternoon snacks with the children and go into the garden and see the plots through the fence.

These have been wonderful moments for everyone and Jacky hoped they would start again once the pandemic was properly over.

Jacky is also hopeful they will be able to resume having the parents for termly coffee mornings, and end of term parties. She said that they take the parents on a tour of the allotments, which has been very popular. The plot holders and committee hold annual produce sales, which parents love to come to and hear the children talk so knowledgeably about the vegetables, plants and environment.

In April 2015, the outdoor waterless toilet was installed on the Bennetts Road Allotment site. This was an environmental innovation at the time, and Jacky said that their Montessori school made a small contribution to the appeal for the lottery funding to purchase and install the toilet.

In 2019, Montessori Schools Association ran a competition to find the school with the most interactive gardening activities and experiences for the children. Horsham Montessori Nursery School won this event and were rightly extremely proud of their achievement. It is also an acknowledgement of the foresight and generous qualities of the Bennetts Road Allotment site in sharing with the community.

Bennetts Road allotment site today

The 2020 pandemic caused many of the allotments community events to be cancelled for two years, and one of the most popular was the annual plant sale. This was established in 2012 and held at the end of May each year. The plant sales have tripled in size and attendance since they began ten years ago. However, in view of the current financial climate, the committee decided not to hold the plant sale in 2022 and were investigating donating surplus produce to local food banks

23. The Bennetts Road Allotments 2018 plant sale. Photo with kind permission of Tracey Leggatt.

24. The Bennetts Road Allotments 2018 plant sale. Photo with kind permission of Tracey Leggatt.

When it did run, the sale was open to the public and was well known for good value in the neighbourhood. Plants sold would include tomatoes, peppers, cucumbers and courgettes, along with allotment produce like rhubarb, flowers, jams and chutneys. Plot holders were behind the stalls and could chat and advise on cultivation. Also on the day, the community area was available for tea, coffee and ever popular home-made cakes.

The plant sale was a major fund raiser for the allotments and the association would expect to make about £700 in profit. In 2018 the event featured in the West Sussex County Times (7th June 2018 edition) and the Chairman Peter Stallibrass

25. Flowers for cutting grown alongside vegetables.

was quoted as saying, 'There's never been a better time to have an allotment. It's cheaper to grow your own food, better quality than you'll get in the shops ... not to mention all the exercise, fresh air and mental well-being ...' Of course, this was exactly what people thought during the pandemic when so many valued the ability to get out into the fresh air safely, so waiting lists for allotments increased, including Bennetts Road allotments.

There have been two workdays a year, usually in March and October, when about fifteen to twenty plot holders come together to undertake necessary maintenance jobs. These might be clearing rubbish from the site, cleaning and tidying the community shed, greenhouses and polytunnel, painting, weeding and hedge trimming, in fact anything else that needs doing, such as work in the wildlife areas and ponds. A lunch is provided in the community area on the two table benches, with, of course, lots of cake.

Acting Chairperson, Kim Leggatt, noted that, 'The allotments are very much an established part of the community, holding plant sales and open days where advice and help is on hand. Thus, the committee have decided to register the site as an Asset of Community Value, which it most definitely is, and should be preserved like all allotment sites, for future community benefit.'

Painting 4. Apples, by Dr Maggie Weir-Wilson

58

Chapter 6: *Birds Farm Allotments*

26. Lynda Cheeseman, Secretary of the Birds Farm Allotment Society tending crops. Photo with kind permission of Lynda Cheeseman.

Birds Farm allotments is a small site of forty plots situated behind Springfield House and off Blunts Way which links Springfield (North Parade) with Rushams Road. The plots are quite small, mostly quarter plots with the remainder being half plots and no full plots. Consequently, there are few structures like sheds, greenhouses or poly tunnels, although they are allowed with permission from the committee. Likewise, fruit trees can only be grown if they are in containers, fruit bushes are fine in the ground. The plot holders are mainly women these days. In 2022 there were twenty-two women and eighteen men. The site has been run since 2014 by the Birds Farm Allotment Society and it is a member of the NSALG.

From the archives

According to a poster produced by King & Chasemore, estate agents, an auction of Birds Farm, three acres described as, '... ripe for development.', was to take place at the Town Hall on Wednesday October 19th 1938. There was an old cottage on the land, let to a Mr Smith, and allotments which produced £30 a year rental from fifty plots. It is not stated who the owners of the land were. However, later records record the original owner as William Burdett Veysey of nearby Springfield Park.

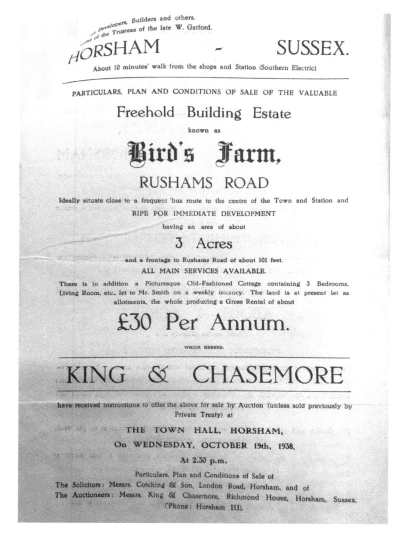

27. Poster advertising auction of land at Birds Farm, October 19th, 1938, WSRO UD/HO/21/2/196.

The Urban District Council received a petition from the allotment holders asking them to exercise their powers of purchase and retain the land for allotments. Thankfully, this is what they did paying £850, having received a loan from the Ministry of Health of £881, which allowed for legal fees and administration.

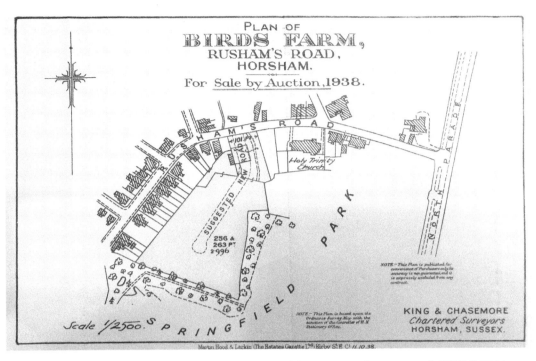

PLAN OF
BIRDS FARM,
RUSHAM'S ROAD,
HORSHAM.
For Sale by Auction, 1938.

Scale 1/2500.

KING & CHASEMORE
Chartered Surveyors
HORSHAM, SUSSEX.

28. Plan of Birds Farm for auction as building plot with a suggested access road. WSRO UD/HO/21/2/196.

The following year it was agreed that the old cottage would be demolished. It was over one hundred years old, had a Horsham stone roof, timber frame and weather boarding, but was felt to be too damp and dilapidated. Poor Mr Smith – presumably the Charlie Smith with pig sties who Nancy Meeten refers to later – who was renting the cottage was not having much luck, as the same year the council asked those tenants who had allotments of ten rods or more to give up half to new plot holders. The council had lost many allotments at Shelley Allotments to the Davis estates and demand for plots was high. Everyone on Birds Farm with large plots, nine in all, agreed to this, apart from Mr Smith who cultivated his plots for the purpose of his trade, he is described as a hawker of vegetables, and had worked the plots from meadow for twenty-four years, which takes the establishment of Birds Farm allotments back to 1915.

In 1940 there were queries over the allotment boundaries on the north-west side which appear to have been enclosed by some of the houses in Rushams Road. One address, 41, had a shed across the boundary and this was subsequently allowed as long as the owner was an allotments holder. It seems that access from the gardens to the allotments had been made by seven properties, and the council was generous in allowing this, but blocked up any garden access that did not belong to plot holders. In autumn 1941 there were worries over five of the oak trees on the boundary near Rushams Road, however it was decided not to remove them as taking them down would cause more damage to the plots than the nuisance caused by them. Nancy remembers that branches from the oaks fell on Mr. Smith's pig sties in the 1950s and again nothing was done.

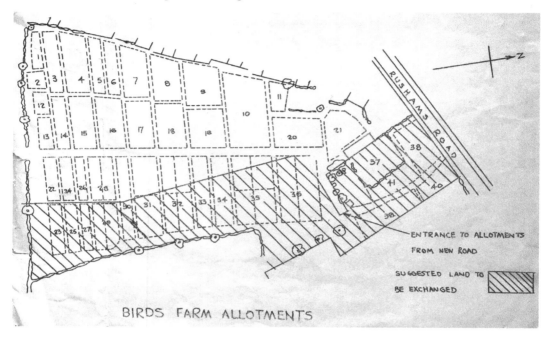

29. Plan, undated, showing suggested land for Davis Estates and the new Blunts Way development. With kind permission of Birds Farm Allotment Society.

In 1948, MP Harris & Co., Builders Merchants, asked the council if they could buy the plot of vacant land in front of the allotments in Rushams Road. They wanted a yard for their materials but given there were many still waiting for plots the council refused. There then seems to be a gap of about twenty years in which either everything was peaceful on Birds Farm and plot holders were getting on with growing, or there are missing documents. I suspect it is the latter, but we next hear about Birds Farm when it was again threatened by building development.

The late 1960s and early 1970s saw Birds Farm allotments first lose almost half their plots to the development of Blunts Way by Davis Estates, secondly any prospect of compensatory plots with the expansion to the building of George Pinion Court – sheltered housing for the British Legion on adjacent council land. At this time, it was felt that many of the allotments were surplus to requirements and so some of the allotments site could be repurposed. A Notice to Quit was served by the council in March 1960 to give the affected allotmenteers twelve months' warning. Davis Estates offered compensation to the council by working to clear an area of land behind Springfield Park that had been a large pond, the one Nancy remembers as having had a boat on it. Davis estates agreed to fill in the pond and return it to good condition, clean and rotovated. However, a block of these new plots, 29 to 48 were to be rented by the council to a market gardener Mr PJ Edwards for flowers, shrubs and fruit trees. A new entrance was then made to access the market garden and the allotments from Blunts Way.

In 1968 the council wrote in a letter that, 'The council's experience is that the use of allotments is declining.' and in the early 70s there were complaints over the state of some of them. Investigations noted that plot one was used as a communal compost heap due to its shaded position. However, there were still requests for allotments and queries over rumours of more building. In August 1974 a local newspaper carried the report that Horsham District Council had approved the development of one and a quarter acres of Birds Farm allotments by the Royal British Legion Housing Association for ex-Service personnel and their dependents in a two-storey building for thirty-five people. The following year, 1975, in reply

to an enquiry for an allotment the council said there was a long waiting list for plots and it was unlikely all those waiting would be allocated plots within the next three years. At this point there were said to be sixteen names on the waiting list.

Nevertheless, in 1976 an application was received by the council for building forty-four, two-person flats with community room, warden's flat and bungalow on land that was to be sold to the British Legion, this building to be named after the local counsellor, George Pinion. Alternative temporary

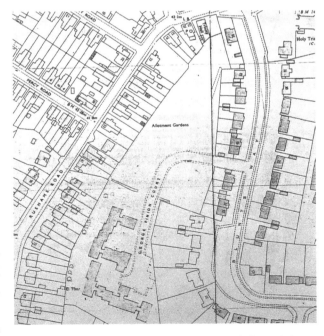

30. Plan of George Pinion Court and remaining Birds Farm allotment site. With kind permission of Birds Farm Allotment Society.

allotments were offered on Hills Farm, past the cemetery off the Guildford Road. Ten years later in 1986 it was suggested that George Pinion Court be extended by twelve to fourteen single person units in the wasteland between the existing buildings and the allotments. It was queried, 'Whether a sufficiently strong case could be established for reducing the area of allotment land.' Mr Christy from Rushams Road wanted to rent a plot, either one, two or three and noted that they had not been cultivated for the last few years. The reply from the Leisure and Recreation Manager was that they were, 'Within the area to be developed and are not available for letting.' So, the expansion of George Pinion Court went ahead.

31. Original track through the site, running towards Rushams Road.

Remembering the past

I spoke to Nancy Meeten, in her mid-eighties and using a mobility scooter to access her allotment plot. She lives on the nearby Victory Road which she has done for many years. She shared her current plot with a friend in the early 2000s but now that friend has moved away and it is just her. Nancy says she will manage the plot for as long as she is able.

Nancy remembers that as a little girl her dad had two plots on Birds Farm, and in the 1940s she was encouraged by her parents to tend it with them. She said that her grandfather had one plot on this site before her dad had his. They used a small pond for water and there were lots of trees. She remembers climbing right to the top of a holly tree when she was seven or eight, and the boy next door also climbed the trees. Nancy recollected that there were some lovely old oak trees and a row of trees halfway down the site called the plantation. Beyond these trees was a much larger pond with a small boat on it.

Nancy's dad had plots forty-one and thirty-nine, which she remembers were near the small pond and the double gates that led onto Rushams Road. This entrance has long since gone, having been built over but the existing path up through the plots is the original one, although smaller in length and with a right-hand bend in it now.

Nancy remembered that her grandfather worked for the blacksmith, whose shop or workplace was where Marlborough Place is now on Rushams Road. The blacksmiths cottage had a Horsham stone roof and was at the top of the allotment site near the small pond and gates. Blunts Way wasn't built then and the allotments stretched as far as the pavements. There were pig sties surrounded by fruit trees on the site owned by a Charlie Smith. According to letters to the council the pig sties had been damaged by falling branches from an oak tree in the early 1950s, but nothing was done about the tree or the sties.

32. Nancy working on her plot. Photo with kind permission of Lynda Cheeseman.

There were very few women with allotments in those days, Nancy could only remember one. She does however remember being deeply impressed by a Mr Morden who used to dig his whole allotment in one evening – a heroic achievement. Her grandfather used to enter produce shows, and her mother helped him keep his runner beans long and straight by wrapping them in damp cloths, so that he won prizes.

A recipe: Sue's beetroot chutney

I spoke to Sue Hammond, Treasurer of the Birds Farm Allotment Society, who has had an allotment on this site for many years. She told me she has been making beetroot chutney and adapting it over the years. She loves beetroot in her cheese or ham sandwiches but is not so keen on vinegar. However, this recipe uses red wine vinegar which Sue says tones down the sharpness produced by a malt vinegar.

Beetroot chutney

3lb (1.3kg) beetroot

1 large onion

1 large cooking apple

12oz (34g) sugar

2tsp ground ginger

1tsp salt

1pt (568 ml) red wine vinegar

33. Sue's beetroot chutney.

1. Cook the beetroot and dice into small pieces.
2. Peel and dice the onion.
3. Peel and dice the apple.
4. Put into a large pan, add the sugar, salt, ginger and vinegar.
5. Bring to the boil and simmer until the ingredients are soft.
6. Ladle into hot, clean, sterilised jars, cover and seal.
7. Label when fully cool.

Notes: The chutney can be spiced up a bit by adding a couple of habanero chillies during cooking.

The chutney, kept in sterilised and sealed jars, should keep for a year in a cool dark place. Once opened keep in the fridge and try to use within four weeks.

Birds Farm allotment site today

Many local allotment sites have oak trees on their boundaries, but Birds Farm have one right in the middle, possibly a lone survivor from the old plantation of trees up the middle of the site. The area underneath it was used as a compost dumping area for many years but this is now discouraged. For safety the council trimmed the tree back in 2017, leaving the large limbs on site as a wildlife habitat. This is now covered with nettles to encourage butterflies and is cut back once a year in early winter. I am informed that a resident fox family also live undisturbed here.

The Birds Farm Allotment Society produces a very informative double page newsletter every year in the Spring. This highlights annual events like coffee mornings and the AGM, encouragement to look after the site well and contribute to the maintenance of paths and community areas. Advice and information on growing are given as are reminders about the responsibilities of allotment holders. Good photographs illustrate the newsletter.

34. The oak tree in 2011 before trimming. Photo with kind permission of Lynda Cheeseman.

There is a communal shed which contains tools and equipment for general use and allotmenteers are encouraged to keep their plots and the general areas in good condition. There are occasional working parties for this purpose. One of the recent tasks was creating a new compost bin for communal grass clippings, as it is surprising how quickly one's own compost bin fills up.

As with most allotment sites in Horsham there is a current waiting list of about three to four years for a plot. This may be because Birds Farm is a small site, well surrounded by residential streets and homes, thus a convenient walk for many. The plots are also smaller and hence more manageable these days for busy families or older folk.

35. The oak tree in 2017 after trimming. Photo with kind permission of Lynda Cheeseman.

Allotment Year

After Winter

I follow the hollow path, sidestepping puddles,
scuffing scents of rain and rotting leaves.

Crumbling bark paths new edged and fixed
with clumps of strong stemmed buttercup.

Sage swamps the still sleeping vine, grey leaves
overpowering each dead dry limb.

Artichoke, now wakeful, stretches heraldic leaves
with continental vigour, eager for spring.

Autumn raspberry struggles to push new fresh growth
through unrelenting couch grass.

Bare branches of cordon apples disappear
under rhubarb's huge horse-hooved leaves.

Late Spring

Magpies strut and dive in freshly turned earth,
air filled with the noise of mowers and stench of petrol.

Comfrey burgeoning in dense thuggish delight
Its blue-pink flowers jostling with bees.

Bruised white petals of pollinated plum, flutter
and fall, job now done, fruit ovaries swelling.

I dig the dry, clay-clumped earth, wishing for fine tilth.
A young frog squeezes from a crack in the soil.

Lone-ranger mask, camouflage trousers, unsteady
on folded legs, moving into safer territory.

Exhausted from digging, I watch two butterflies settle,
then spiral up, orange wings against the sun.

Autumn

Wasps worry the last raspberry remnants
Deep-red drops of soft decay

Crouching apple trees full of fruit;
I test each one, turning, twisting.

Spiders sling ropes like mountain climbers
and abseil down runner bean canes.

Globe artichoke, silver leaves now shrivelled,
its glorious purple thistle flower attracting bees.

Pumpkin and squash nestle close to the ground,
my thoughts quickly turn to warm soups and stews.

I take my harvest and lock the shed.

Painting 5. Apples, by Dr Maggie Weir-Wilson

Chapter 7: *Chesworth Allotments*

36. The main gate off Arun Way.

Chesworth allotment site is a large one, the largest of the ten town allotment sites at over 10.2 acres (4.128 ha) and has 150 plots. The site is leased from Horsham District Council on a rolling ten-year agreement with rent reviews every five years. It will next be up for renewal in 2027. HDC give a reduction on the lease for self-management of the site by the Chesworth Allotment Society, run by a dedicated committee. Rent for an individual full plot in 2021 was £66, plus affiliate membership of the National Allotment Society.

37. Path down to allotments from Gorings Mead.

38. Aerial photo of the allotment site looking south towards Chesworth Farm, with kind permission of Ian Shaw.

Chesworth Allotments
South of Brighton Road
Horsham.
Scale: 1/1250 approx.

39. Plan of Chesworth Allotment Site showing 150 full plots. With thanks to Alison Paul, secretary of Chesworth Allotment Society.

The site is bounded on the two upland southern sides by Chesworth Farm, a council site managed as farm land, and on the northern lower side by houses. Access is either from the Brighton Road via a footpath from Gorings Mead, or vehicle access from Arun Way. There are three locked gates onto the site, one from Gorings Mead and two from Arun Way. In recent years it has been necessary to increase the security around the site and now Gorings Mead has two sets of locked gates. There is anti-climb paint on most gates and solar powered CCTV.

From the archives

There is evidence from the records office in Chichester that in 1922 the council was renting 7.716 acres for allotments in the Chesworth Farm area from the Eversfield Trustees. At this date they agreed to rent another field of three acres one rod from the same trustees for the purposes of more allotments. The new field was referred to as the New Town allotments. It was leased for £23 3s for nineteen years and the cost of conversion to allotments was £17 10s which included laying out, pegs, a sleeper bridge over the ditch, sixty yards of five-foot fencing and making good the holes in hedging with barbed wire.

In 1928 a letter was sent from the secretary of the Chesworth Allotment Society to the council asking for a reduction in rents as they were finding their allotment holders switching to Hills allotments, which were apparently cheaper. They also asked if the council could actually buy this land. The council asked the Denne Park Estate if they would sell but this only resulted in an extension to the lease to 1949. However, on 20th February 1929 at the Town Hall the outlying portion of the Denne Park Estate, 258 acres were offered for sale. Lot 2 of the auction were two enclosures of allotment ground forming ten acres three rods and thirty-four poles, with access from the Brighton Road. The council did its sums and the allotments were bought for £650 with £20 costs, the total amount being loaned from the Ministry of Health.

Subsequently, the council received letters of complaints from plot holders about loose cattle eating their cabbages and trampling over celery beds, so clearly the hedging was not secure between the fields. As ever, there were also complaints about children playing on the allotments, and later in April 1930, complaints about the dumping of metal and rubbish on the New Town allotments with even the police becoming involved.

The dumping of rubbish on the footpath to Chesworth allotment came to light again in May 1935 when police checked out reports and found carts, manure, peat, and an old motor car had been dumped by two

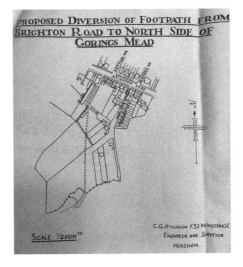

40. Map showing dotted line of public footpath across the allotment site, and proposed alteration in red. WSRO catalogue UD/HO/21/2/185.

73

neighbours. These two neighbours promised police they wouldn't do it again. However, old bits of iron were later found in the ditches and it was suggested children had been dumping the metal there. The police suggested the allotments put up a notice against dumping.

There were some pig sties on Chesworth allotments. In 1932 Mr Wickens had asked permission from the council to keep pigs at the top end of the allotments away from the houses. This was granted, along with a rent reduction so that the society could allow the unemployed to use unused plots rent free. Six years later there was a request for hard core to improve the road to the plots with pig sties, which were rented by seven members of the Chesworth Allotment Society. This was agreed, and a year later there was a request for water to be laid to Mr Chapman's pig sties, for which the council agreed to pay half the cost.

In 1938, FC Boxall, builders and decorators, enquired whether the council would be interested in buying their land near Gorings Mead, on the other side of the stream, for allotments. The council replied thank you, but no, they had enough with their ongoing negotiations for the Shelley and Clarence Road sites. There followed protracted attempts by the council to alter the footpath from Boxall's land which ran diagonally across the allotments from the Brighton Road to the north side of Gorings Mead, eventually this was agreed, with the start of it now being known as Boxall Walk.

41. Photo of the lower first gate off Arun Way, 1970s. Image copyright © Ray Luff, Horsham Museum.

42. Photo of the upper second gate off Arun Way, 1970s. Image copyright © Ray Luff, Horsham Museum.

Post war there were further negotiations with Boxall who wanted to build thirty-three homes in Gorings Mead with the intention of renting seventeen of them to ex-service men. However, problems with an access road and sewer connections meant the council turned down this proposal. There was an appeal and the council then offered to buy just over four acres of Boxall's land for allotments due to the fact that they thought they would lose three and a half acres of existing allotments which were planned for residential purposes. After more negotiations, Boxall eventually agreed to accept £525 for his land and a draft contract was drawn up. However, when the council approached Chesworth Allotment Society to take over this land they refused, saying there was now little demand for more allotments. The whole scheme was therefore dropped. The Chesworth site remained just the two original fields it had been back in the 1920s.

A rather good story emerged from the archives, as they occasionally do. In June 1950, it seems that gooseberries from two bushes had been stolen, plus a bundle of bean sticks, from a plot on Chesworth allotments. Arrangements were made for a local police constable to attend the allotments at 4.00 a.m. to keep watch on the Tuesday, nothing happened. On the Wednesday, 14th June at 5.15 a.m., the culprit, a Mr Smith from Bennetts Road, was apprehended stealing strawberries. He went before the local Magistrates on the 11th July 1950 and was fined £5. Those were the days! No chance today that the police would stake out my Chesworth plot and arrest the villain who has been taking my much anticipated first globe artichokes and beautiful French golden gage plums.

Remembering the past

I spoke to Beryl Jarvis, volunteer at Horsham Museum, who remembered Chesworth allotments from the 1970s. She spoke fondly of it being a very friendly place. It was full of older men who had lots of advice to give on growing veg. One piece of advice was slightly different - how to keep your feet warm - fill your wellington boots with crumpled newspaper, it keeps the feet really toastie in winter! She remembered only a couple of women working plots and just a few sheds. It was very local with most plot holders walking or cycling. She remembers that they all worked the full ten rods, and quite a few had two or three plots. Beryl did in fact divide her plot in half to share with a friend. This is something I did with mine a couple of years ago when it all became a bit too much.

One story that came from a Horsham in Bloom judge, was that on inspecting the Chesworth allotments in the early 2000s, one judge noticed some herbaceous plants growing under a cloche that he had never seen before, apparently it was cannabis! However, seeing that it was a small amount clearly only for personal use, the judges walked on.

Chesworth's famous Italian allotmenteers

Many will remember Angelo Pallidino, a frequent winner of Horsham District Council's Best Kept Allotment competition in the 1990s. He grew a large variety of Italian vegetables and herbs on his Chesworth plot. Often, he would bring a selection of his tomatoes, peppers and chillies to the award ceremony in Park House to the delight of the judges. The judges visited each of the ten Horsham allotment sites that were in their remit and looked at the general appearance of the plots and surrounding paths, pest and disease control, weed control, methods of cultivation, and of course, crop quality and yield. To get to such a high standard required lots of hard work and dedication. The competitions and awards were run by Horsham in Bloom but this organisation is sadly no longer active.

I was lucky enough to have a phone conversation with an elderly Italian allotmenteer, Francesco De Amtomis, who had a plot for many years at Chesworth. He grew potatoes, onions, garlic, French and borlotti beans, and brassicas. He won first prize in a competition for his cabbages and was known as the 'Cabbage King'. Generously he gave his £100 winnings to the local hospital. He is a firm believer that fresh vegetables are, 'the best food you can eat', and he is undoubtedly correct.

I had thought that maybe it was the Prisoner of War camps at Coolham, Mannings Heath and Billingshurst that accounted for the vibrant Italian community in Horsham. However, Francesco said that although as prisoners they had worked well on farms, perhaps unsurprisingly, most went home after the war. It was the later search for good paying employment in the 1960s that brought many Italian people back to the UK for work, particularly from central and southern Italy.

Francesco himself had been working in a mine in Belgium in the 1950s when he came on holiday to visit his sister who was working at a school in Horsham. He met one of the managers from Warnham Brickworks, who he recognised from being in the same hospital when they were both wounded during the war. He was offered a job and so got a work permit and joined many of the other Italian men working in the brickworks in Warnham, Southwater, Capel, Lingfield and Dorking. These small brickworks became the Sussex & Dorking Brick Company which was bought by Redland bricks in 1958. Francesco estimated that there were about fifty to one hundred Italian families in this area at that time. However, when their work contracts ended after four or five years, the majority returned home to an Italy which was becoming more prosperous.

Giuseppe Iebba, or 'Joe' as he is more usually known, has a plot and a half near the shop and toilet on Chesworth allotments. He told me that he came to England from southern Italy, near Naples. As a young man he had been working in Switzerland on demolition jobs, but through an aunt and uncle in England he found out about work opportunities here. So, in the mid-1960s he obtained a four-year contract working as a school handyman in Roffey, gardening, building, and general maintenance. He was soon joined in England by his parents, his father getting a job with Redland Bricks and meeting other Italian people who had left southern Italy for work here.

43. Joe with lettuce seedlings near his plot.

Through meeting other local Italian families, Joe's dad got an allotment at Chesworth and of course Joe helped him cultivate it. They got to know the ten or fifteen families in the area and when Joe's dad passed away, Joe took over his allotment. He no longer has his father's plot, but his current plots are ones he has cultivated for over four years. Joe grows proper Italian Oregano, heritage Italian tomatoes and from the longer varieties he makes tomato passata, usually about two hundred litres a year. He also grows Italian globe artichokes which he picks small, stuffs with breadcrumbs and bacon and then gently simmers.

44. Joe's greenhouse grown Italian tomatoes in 2021.

There are now only four Italian families represented on Chesworth allotments. Gone are the days when the men from Redland brickworks could take on the big Chesworth allotments due to their work shifts of four days on and four days off. Some, like Salvatore, cultivate plots near the second gate and grow vines,

45. Geraldo Ricca, (or 'Gerry' as he is known) by his productive plot.

but mainly the Italian families import grapes from Italy and make wine from them. According to Joe it results in a sweeter taste due to the Italian soil and climate. Salvatore certainly knows about fruit and has helped me with advice and pruning various trees. Next to the shop is another Italian, Gerry, whose one and a half plots are always beautifully kept and produce an excellent range of vegetables.

Joe told me his best growing tip, 'There is nothing to beat properly composted cow manure dug into your soil every year.'

Chesworth allotment site today

Ex-chairman Mike Dancy told me that the idea to provide a proper toilet came from the successful application made by Bennetts Road allotment site. Liz Thorns masterminded the Chesworth grant application and Bob Downes organised volunteers to do the digging and construction. Thus, the new eco-friendly compostable and accessible toilet was opened by local MP Jeremy Quin in May 2018.

Mike also told me that the need to upgrade the old shop/wooden store was necessary due to its state of dilapidation. This, along with an increase in business made it very labour intensive to manage. Originally, plans were drawn up for a new complex inside the first gate in from Arun Way to take advantage of mains drainage, electricity and water near that area, but a more central location was eventually chosen to make access better for all.

The committee came upon the Hepworth's shop building by chance, as Hepworth's would have abandoned it when they moved from Station Yard to Brinsbury. John Tewson was instrumental in negotiating for its release to Chesworth allotments. A team of volunteers dismantled it and moved it adjacent to vacant plot 7A, whilst planning was approved and the existing old wooden allotment building was emptied of stock. The wooden store was then demolished which allowed eight concrete foundation pads to be constructed for the steel building legs and the new building assembled around the old shop. On completion the old shop was demolished. It was hoped that the new building would be fifty per cent shop and fifty per cent workshop but that has yet to transpire. It is currently open on a Sunday morning, staffed by volunteers, and selling fertilisers, compost, ground cover and canes.

46. Frame of the new shop erected over the original shop by volunteers Bob Downes, Dave Harry, Derek Williams and Robin Atfield.

47. The volunteer weekend working party in the hot summer of 2022.
Photo from Facebook: Chesworth Allotment Society.

There is a good water supply with taps and dipping tanks throughout the site. Maintenance jobs, such as the trimming of hedgerows is undertaken by volunteers in regular work parties. Scrap metal has been collected and sold for a small sum, but there is always the problem of non-metal items being dumped, with even an old washing machine appearing! A temporary bonfire plot has been established to deal with dry material. Care has to be taken with any communal or individual burning due to smoke which can be a nuisance to the nearby houses. It is requested that wind direction is always checked before beginning to burn, and for ease of this a windsock flies up above the car parking area off the first gate in Arun Way. If the big orange sock is pointing away from the houses towards Chesworth Nature Reserve, then burning can go ahead.

The bunker

Up in the top western corner of the allotment site is an overgrown area surrounded by concrete posts and high wire fencing. If the curious plot holder peers in, they will be able to see amongst the vegetation a small concrete square box. This is the remains of one of almost nine hundred Royal Observer Corps (ROC) Cold War early warning systems, two of which were in Horsham, this one and a larger group headquarters now demolished. They were established throughout the UK from the early 1960s to the early 1990s. Their sole purpose was to warn the local population of impending doom i.e., a nuclear attack.

48. What can be seen today (2021) of the entrance to the bunker.

49. A photo from 2009 by Mark Russell showing the open uncapped entrance to the bunker. © Subterranea Britannica/Mark Russell.

The concrete box had a green metal lid that opened onto a metal ladder which led down to an underground bunker. Here three observers could communicate directly with their group controller plus other ROC posts. The main business was to receive the nuclear warning from RAF Strike Command and so enable a local warning to be given from the bunker.

50. The interior of the bunker taken by Mark Russell probably in 2009, before it was sealed, other photos were taken by Nick Catford. © Subterranea Britannica/Mark Russell.

51. The interior of the bunker taken by Mark Russell probably in 2009, before it was sealed, other photos were taken by Nick Catford. © Subterranea Britannica/Mark Russell.

A group called Subterranea Britannica are fascinated with British underground remains and have listed on their website many different types of underground sites which includes the Chesworth Allotment bunker. They list it as opened in 1961 and closed in 1991 when the Cold War ended. It appears it was explored by members of this group in 1997. At this time, they reported that the enclosure was heavily overgrown, however it was possible to climb down inside the bunker and it was found that much remained. They reported seeing, '… shelf, bench, cupboards, a chest of drawers, wiring, rack of shelves, paperwork, maps, mattresses, two folding chairs and various other items including four unopened packets of throw away panties.' Photos of the bunker, inside and out, were taken around 2009 by Nick Catford and Mark Russell which thankfully records it all for posterity. A later entry in 2019 by John Gibson noted that there had been repeated vandalism and that the top had been capped with concrete so no access was then possible. This is how it has stayed, becoming increasingly overgrown and attracting puzzled stares.

52. Bird box on wildlife plot 78a Photo with kind permission of Rob Robertson.

The wildlife plots

In late 2020 a few of the committee led by Rob Robertson got together as a subgroup to consider what could be done on the site to encourage wildlife. It was recognised that a greater variety of species can help allotment growers as a natural form of pest control, as well as pollinators. In addition, our own wellbeing is improved by the sights and sounds of plentiful wildlife. Of course, some species are more welcome to gardeners than others but a balanced environment allows us to live with and tolerate these.

53. Young smooth newt found beneath ground cover. Photo with kind permission of Rob Robertson.

It is important to note that the allotment site is next door to Chesworth Farm Local Wildlife Site and so the area is particularly rich in wildlife. Tim Thomas, the ecology expert from Chesworth Farm visited the allotment site in 2021 to give advice on encouraging wildlife on two dedicated plots, plus in the perimeter hedges, scrub and trees.

The committee has set aside two plots as wildlife plots, that is plot 78a and 54a. These plots had been difficult to cultivate on the western edge of the site under oak trees and were almost wild already. The plan is to include a pond on plot 78a, and on both plots to have wildflower areas with mammal and reptile refuges. Bird boxes are already in place and there are plans for bat boxes, and hopefully owl boxes, in the future.

In addition to the plots there is a register of the types of wildlife spotted around the site and it is hoped everyone will get into the habit of reporting sightings. There is a camera trap ready to snap interesting visitors and it is hoped a bat detector will be available at some point. So far, since recording began, thirty-six different types of birds have been spotted, nine different types of mammals and five reptiles and amphibians. It is planned to add insects and butterflies, plants, flowers, trees and fungi to the register in time.

John Tewson and his vine plot

54a. John Tewson with his vines.

John first took on a plot and a half at Chesworth thirteen years ago with his daughter, growing the usual vegetables. John worked for the old Horsham brewery, King & Barnes before it closed in 2000 and he was made redundant. However, with enterprising friends from the old brewery and led by Andy Hepworth, John helped to set up the new brewery of Hepworth. Whilst there he made friends with a freewheeling man who had worked on his own vineyard in New Zealand. The man had moved often to work in other breweries and vineyards in Europe and had useful contacts in the wine trade. This got John thinking about a vine plot and so seven years ago he took on another large plot in the middle of the Chesworth allotment site and set about growing vines.

He knew he wanted to grow a red grape that he could turn into a decent wine, and he knew what he liked, having holidayed in Italy and Greece, and having always drunk the local wine. His friend contacted a nursery in northern Germany who sent vines in bundles of twenty-five over to this country. John was therefore able to take delivery, for next to nothing, of seventy-five vines known as VB/39, based on a Cabinet Sauvignon which grew in the similar climatic conditions of northern Germany. Research on the internet told John how to plant the vines and secure them on their wires. He was to only let them grow to five foot (1.5m) and prune them when dormant, December or January and then harvest in October, depending on the ripening. Due to his background in the brewing industry, he knew all about the importance of sugar content and specific gravity with relation to alcohol. He told me that he feels the growing part is relatively easy, it's the making of a good drinkable wine that is the tricky part.

His first year of production was 2018, 160 bottles of he says, somewhat average wine. The second year was better quality although the grapes were caught just before some nasty mildew set in. John thought that vintage had improved with keeping. Then came 2020, a write off due to the late frosts taking the blossom. The following year, 2021 was looking promising until the foxes ate all the grapes off his vines, despite protection. *Subsequent information has been that foxes are not that keen on grapes and the more likely culprits were local badgers.*

We wait with anticipation for the '22 Chesworth vintage. When John does eventually get his next harvest of grapes, the wine will be made in his daughter's garage in big stainless steel ninety litre vats, recycled, as only a brewery engineer like John can, from a left-over pipe and with quite a bit of welding.

54b. John Tewson's vines.

Chesworth Community Allotment

Chesworth Community Allotment was set up in the summer of 2012 by an enthusiastic group of Transition Horsham members. The Chesworth Allotment Society committee agreed to allow the use of a large plot on the northern edge of the site, bounded by oak trees, a stream and hidden paths. To begin with the number of weeds were enough to weaken the resolve of the keenest volunteer, but the first working party on Sunday, 8th July 2012, got stuck in and by that autumn there were five dug beds and an apple and pear tree had been discovered.

55. Clearing weeds in the second working party, 2012.

56. Erecting the shed donated by Newbridge Nursery.

57. Laying the path on the community allotment.

A large shed was kindly donated by Nigel West, Managing Director of Newbridge Nursery when it was independent, this gave a very valuable warm dry space for tools and equipment, as well as somewhere for volunteers to have a cup of tea. Other local companies then got involved. In 2014, Rudridge, the civil engineering and groundwork material specialist based in Horsham, launched a Community Project Campaign and the community allotment benefitted from this through a donation of the company's expertise and materials. It was thus possible to make the plot more accessible through the laying of a path and patio plus the creation of two raised beds. This same year the community allotment was chosen as one of the Waitrose *Green Token* community groups and benefitted by £494. A grant was also received from Southern Water Authority. Amongst other things compost was obtained to improve the soil, and water harvesting equipment was bought and installed.

A greenhouse that had been abandoned on one of the other plots in the winter of 2013 was kindly allowed by the committee to be taken by the community allotment and erected next to the new path and patio. Thus, tomatoes could now be happily grown.

A small pond already existed on the plot, 2m by 1m, clay lined but with little or no wildlife. So, in January 2014, a report was prepared by Peter Birchall, aka 'Pete the Pond', who made recommendations to enlarge it and put in sloping shallows and logs near the edges and add aquatic plants, this was done and frogspawn was seen in early 2015. A liner was later added but by 2020 it was no longer holding water. It had silted up and the aquatic plants had grown too big. During a dry spell in that spring, the pond was dug to at least twice the size and made a fraction deeper with shelves and sloping sides. A new liner was fitted and the perennial weeds around the edges were removed. Once it was refilled with water, new pond plants and marginals were added, plus stones and logs around the edges. It looked again like a natural pond, and now has newts and water boatman.

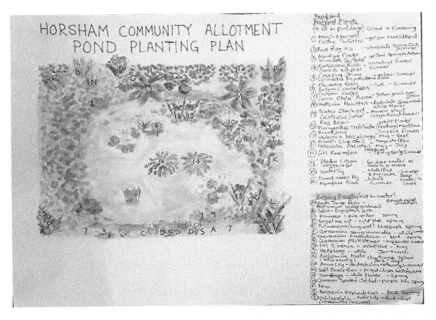

58. Horsham Community Allotment, pond planting plan, With kind permission from Rose McKinney.

59. A summer barbeque on the community plot in July 2014.

Volunteer teams have increased from meeting once a Saturday in summer, with the occasional Wednesday, to three times a week. These working parties are friendly social events for those in the community who wish to try their hand at growing, learning what to do if necessary, and taking home some fresh organic produce that they can be proud of. A regular and enjoyable event has been the summer barbeque to which the rest of Chesworth allotmenteers are usually invited to see the progress on the plot and chat to the volunteers, some of whom go on to

60. Work party in winter 2021, showing new raised beds and enlarged pond with new liner.

61. Rob and Cath Robertson building new compost bays to keep up with demand.

have allotments themselves. There have also been Open Days. The first was on a Saturday in April 2015 when all were welcome to talk to the team, drink tea, eat cake and have a tour of the allotment.

Most recent developments have been assisted with a grant from HDC to encourage diversity and accessibility in community projects. This paid, amongst other things, for the materials in the new raised beds and heritage fruit trees. The three apple trees chosen all have a local history. One tree is a Dr Hogg, grown first at Leonardslee in the mid-1800s and named after the Victorian pomologist, Robert Hogg, who called it a, 'First rate baking apple.'. The other two trees are First and Last described by Hogg as, 'Much grown in the northern part of the county around Horsham, the flesh crisp and fine with a slightly sweet flavour.' (Short, 2012).

Chesworth Allotments committee continues to innovate and the latest idea is to have a community compost plot. Rob and Cath Robertson have been working to create bays out of wooden pallets so that plot holders can put their weeds and green waste in one bay, then when full it can be turned and covered to rot down. The compost will then be sold back to allotmenteers at a reasonable price to support the site. This has been welcomed as a great idea and has started to be used immediately and with enthusiasm.

Postscript

Just as this book was going to press I was handed some archival material that had been languishing in a loft for many years. They appeared to have been originally in the possession of a secretary of Chesworth Allotment Society, J.W. Holmwood of Oakhill Road. These archives consisted of two hand written books and a file of various papers and notes, all concerned with Chesworth Allotment Society.

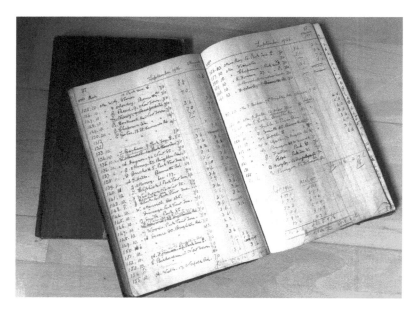

62. The two recently received archive books. The open one shows the lists of plots, with relevant details.

The first of the books is a twenty-year record of committee meetings from January 1924 to 1944. The other book initially records allotment plot numbers, area, plot holder's name and address, and rental paid from March 1927 through the war until March 1949. An interesting note at the end of the 1939-40 listing is a note of five plot holders 'called to colours', i.e. joined the armed forces. Of these five a Miss Cox of Cambridge Road, who had worked plot 78 since at least 1927, was noted as joining the Women's Land Army, where no doubt her experience in allotmenteering would have been well used. The detailed listing ceases in 1944, and working from the rear of the book backwards it continues with balance sheet accounts from 1938 to 1949, the balances increasing slightly over that time from £118 to £288.

Looking into the file of assorted papers the theft of fruit in 1950 was confirmed by a summons to Court for a witness, the secretary of the Society, Mr T. G. Elphick. Hand written letters in very faint ink seem to indicate that Mr. Smith, the culprit's father, kept pigs on the allotments and was asked to cease. The pig sties were subsequently removed and the concrete bases broken up in 1970 to enable the ground to be let as allotment plots.

Papers from the 1950s show that the government was interested in allotment food production as there was a request for completion of a Survey of Allotment Production, plus the continuation of a Scheme for the Award of Certificates of Merit by the Ministry of Agriculture and Fisheries which rewarded the skills and management of individual plot holders in producing food throughout the year. Among these papers are also warnings for Colorado Beetle, encouraging awareness of this potato pest.

March 1969 marked Chesworth Allotment Society's affiliation to the National Allotments and Garden Society. Thus, the file includes much literature from this national society including issues around the Thorpe Report. There is an interesting cutting from the West Sussex County Times dated 7th November, 1969 responding to the Thorpe Report's suggestion for the establishment of leisure gardens rather than allotments. In particular reference to Horsham town the journalist writes that in its 'pattern of concentrated development and more sophisticated approach toward hobbies, the leisure garden could prove a useful and pleasant alternative to the fast-dying allotments area'.

There is note of participation in the 1966 Agricultural Lime Scheme, two tons being delivered to Chesworth allotments for spreading. A gardening club had been set up to sell discounted fertilizer, insecticide, bean and pea stick and other goods, much like the society's shop today. The 1960s saw the negotiations for land surrendered to the Horsham Urban District Council for rental to the Air Ministry and the building of the ROC post. Finally, there is a very small booklet of Chesworth Tenancy Bye-Laws from 1959-1973 covering seventeen rules about arrears, nuisance, proper cultivation, building and dogs.

Painting 6. Tomatoes, by Dr Maggie Weir-Wilson

Chapter 8: *Clarence Road Allotments*

63. The gate into Clarence Road allotments site from Clarence Road.

The layout of the Clarence Road allotments site is an odd shape with no uniform paths and sizes of plots, the numbering system also being somewhat bizarre. This is due to its history of three sites combined into one and much of the original land being sold off for housing in the 1960s. Before the Covid pandemic there were fifty-six individual plots with forty-four plot holders, but due to the increasing demand some plots have been split so that there are now sixty individual plots and fifty plot holders. The area of the site is 1.767 acres or 0.715 ha., which is 215 rods altogether.

64. Map of plots on the Clarence Road allotment site July 2022 devised by John Connolly and available on the society's website www.clarenceroadallotments.org

As with the other town allotments, the site is rented from Horsham District Council but

65. Bob Bogucki's bug house with lots of nooks and crannies.

66. The start of the 2022 September barbeque in the community area.

managed since 2014 by a committee, the Clarence Road Allotment Society. The lease from the council is due to be renewed in April 2025. Rental to plot holders is worked out at £8.25 per rod (20.5 sq. meters) as all the plots vary considerably in size. Any plot holder wanting to put up a shed or greenhouse has to ask the committee for permission and anything over ten by eight foot (3 x 2.4 metres) the committee has to ask the council. As with most allotments committees they are members of the National Allotment and Leisure Gardens Society with the benefits that brings to plot holders. There is of course a waiting list for plots but not perhaps as long as some, in mid-2022 it stood at ten.

Quite a diversity of wildlife has been spotted on the site, the ditch adds a damp dimension to the habitat. Bob Bogucki has built a very impressive large bug house on his second plot to encourage pollinators. One empty plot in the eastern corner under large oak trees is where beehives were kept for a while, however this project was abandoned given that bees in close proximity to people and noise does not work. The old bee plot has now been set aside for wildlife led by Jenny Altamirano Smith who wrote the following:

'Harriet Mayo created a dead hedge behind the hazel tree, along the Elm Grove side. Then, inspired by the wildlife garden at Chesworth Farm, plot holder Jenny Altamirano Smith met with Tony Cook from the Chesworth Farm project and drew up plans for the plot to encourage native species of plants and wildlife. In the summer of 2022, the first working party met in the rain to clear away the invasive snowberry and make space for native plants and flowers to grow. Another work party is planned for the Autumn and seasonally after that, to plant native hedgerow flowers, set some standing logs and build another bug hotel to rival Bob's.

'Eventually, it is hoped that children and families who visit the wildlife plot will be able to connect with nature at a small scale and get ideas for wildlife friendly features that they could include in their own gardens.'

The two plots, which are now the community area, were originally worked by a Frenchman called Claude, who was helping to look after his elderly mother-in-law here in Horsham. When she passed away, he left and returned to France, leaving a shed and plots that were increasingly difficult to cultivate being under the shadow of two oak trees. Thus, these two plots became a community area, with benches donated by Horsham District Council, a greenhouse donated by a Clarence Road resident, and two sheds in which to store equipment.

The area is now being used again after the pandemic, for barbecues twice a year, a bonfire in November and monthly coffee and cake gatherings which have been running since Autumn 2021. One half of this community area has recently been cultivated again by a new family who wanted to try their hand at allotmenteering. Coincidently, one of them is French, thus the plot has turned full circle. The two sheds have now been replaced by one larger shed, kindly donated to the society, and is a good example of recycling in action within a community.

67. John Connolly's plot.

Piped water was laid in 1980 after a ten-year delay by the council who felt it was too expensive a project, John Connolly notes on the website that in 1970 it would only have cost £35. However, now there are four taps with tanks for dipping.

From the archives

The 1840 Tithe Map of Horsham shows a large field east of New Street, before Clarence Road and Elm Grove were even thought of, divided into allotment plots,

93

rented by the Labourers' Friend Society and owned by an Elizabeth Bridger. These would be the forerunner of today's Clarence Road allotment site, if not in the current position then very close by. A later County Series OS Map of 1911 shows Clarence Road partially lined with houses and the current allotment site with some building on Oakhill Road, giving it its unique shape. A footpath runs south over more allotment land and another large area to the east also marked as allotments which has certainly been built over since then.

County Series 1:2500 2nd Rev 1911

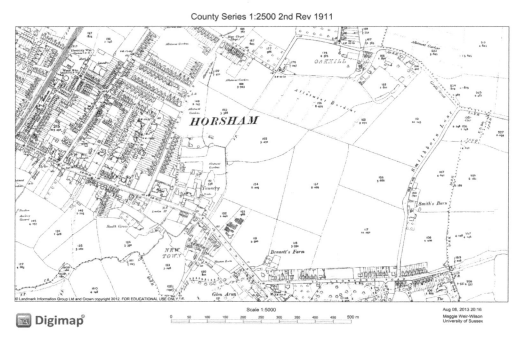

68. Horsham town, East, showing allotment plots, reproduced with permission of Edina Historic Digimap. © Crown Copyright and Landmark Information Group Limited, 2022. All rights reserved. OS County Series, 1.2500, 2nd Revision, 1911.

There is a book in the West Sussex Records Office recording the rentals from land 1883-1912 of the Trustees of Col. Charles Bridger which mentions allotment ground and allotment gardens, some at £6 a year and others at £10 per half year. It appears some land was sold but in June 1910 it is noted that rental from Horsham Allotment Gardens at Clarence Road, varies from £15, to £10 and £6 a plot, payable in advance. There seem to be thirty plots and ten named tenants all living in nearby streets. Henry Parker appears to have three plots plus land at the rear of Clarence Road of three and a half acres. He is later reported as bankrupt and the land taken over by his son Edward. In 1930 there are ten plots and eleven tenants.

From Horsham Urban District Council (HUDC) archives the first mention of Clarence Road allotments is in a letter signed by twelve allotment holders in August 1934 asking the council to prevent the allotments being turned into a Public Right of Way between Clarence Road and the cinder path leading to Elm Grove. They complained also to openings in the hedges onto Oakhill Road and thus the allotments were overrun with dogs, bicycles, motorbikes and prams. A year later it was noted that the allotmenteers were erecting their own boundaries and being somewhat creative with old iron railings and bedsteads, presumably as nothing had been done to prevent trespassers. The council said part of the land had been sold by the owners, which was not the council, for development, and the rest was owned by a number of Trustees who said they had no assets to improve the boundaries.

More trouble came in the autumn of 1935 when near to the footpath from Oakhill Road to Highlands Road large bonfires on an empty plot had damaged an allotmenteers vegetables, including her Brussels sprouts. These dangerous fires appeared to be from general refuse. Boundaries continued to be a problem with a request coming in 1937 to sell the unsightly old iron bedsteads to raise money for a fence. The council replied that as these had been put up by plot holders, they were not the councils to sell and anyway the land was likely to be sold for development.

On the 18th October 1938 a special meeting of the HUDC Allotments Committee convened, and the Oakhill Allotments site (or Clarence Road) was considered, amongst others. The land required for the Brighton Road Housing Scheme would dispossess 110 allotment holders. It was therefore decided that their leases would be extended and the housing postponed until the following year. By then, war was in the wind. Thus, under the 1937 Physical Training and Recreation Act, 1.6 acres of allotment land were bought by the council on 31st January 1941 for direct letting as allotment plots, and a further 0.89 acres were added on 7th November 1945.

Much later, on 6th February 1975, a memo was sent internally within the council querying the name of the allotment site. It refers to the three allotment sites all contained within one piece of land and each called after their bordering streets of Clarence Road, Elm Grove and Oakhill Road. The suggestion was that the whole be renamed as one large site, to be known as Elm Grove Allotments. Clearly there must have been some disagreement as the site is now known as Clarence Road Allotments.

Remembering the past

In the summer of 2021, when we were allowed out between lockdowns, I visited Clarence Road Allotments and met Bob Bogucki who has a large plot at the entrance to the site. He introduced me to Mick Manktelow and his son Michael. Mick is in his late eighties and had obtained his first allotment at Clarence Road in 1957. He remembered a much bigger area of allotments going down as far as St John's Close, almost double the size of the site today. He talked of apple and pear orchards all around, echoed no doubt in the name of Orchard Road, and the sound of nightingales singing from the branches.

69. Digger removing the soil and debris bank in 2016. Photo with kind permission of Bob Bogucki.

70. One of the four extra allotment plots on that site in 2021. Photo with kind permission of Bob Bogucki.

Mick recalled a stream running south from the small lakes by Depot Road across the allotments and down to where the tannery was by Tanyard Close, off the Brighton Road. This stream was eventually diverted to run in pipes underground, but there is still a ditch on the allotment site which is liable to flooding.

As you enter the allotment site, on the left-hand side, there used to be a large bank of soil. Mick remembered that it was here that old Jack Redford used to dump the road sweepings, brought by horse and cart, onto the allotment site. This way a large bank of sweepings built up over the years. Then about six years ago the council cleared it away and the area is now four extra allotments. The soil is a bit different to the rest of the site, sandier and full of pebbles, but all sorts of broken debris can still be found in it including broken clay pipes. Even a second world war bomb and shell were found, not live thankfully.

Mick remembered the remand home on Oakhill Road where boys used to jump over the wall onto the allotments and he used to chase them back. He told me that Christopher Craig the sixteen-year-old accomplice of nineteen-year-old Derek Bentley spent time in this home before he and Bentley committed their ill-fated burglary of a Croydon warehouse in November 1952 when Craig shot a police officer dead. Due to his age, it was Bentley who was hung for it and Craig who went to prison for ten years, later marrying and becoming a plumber.

Mick says he worked hard on his allotment. After a day's work for George Potter, building contractor, and then for himself as GMW Builders, he would work on his four allotment plots evenings and weekends. All digging was done by hand and he could do ten spits (a spit is the depth of one spade) in half an hour each evening. He would manure his plots every year with cow dung which came in an open truck from Chesworth Farm. Mick grew all the usual things, potatoes, French and runner beans, Brussels sprouts, so he was able to feed his family, who, he says, loved jacket potatoes the best.

There has been little trouble over the years on the plots, although Mick did remember someone coming and stealing his pea sticks and, on another occasion, someone else took water for the cabbage plants Mick was growing at his home nearby. He also remembered a man, Tom Brockhurst, who was suffering from regular theft and so decided to hide in a compost bin and then pop out to catch the thief red-handed. This worked, but apparently, he scared the thief half to death!

A long-standing plot holder of thirty-one years is Peter Challis, still working his plot with enthusiasm and with many memories. He told me that all those years ago when he started there was not a woman or child to be seen on the allotments. It was mainly old men, negative in approach, largely unsociable and opposed to change, but evidently able to forecast the weather from changes in wind direction alone! Things did however gradually get better. Many plot holders are now families, several from Europe and beyond. Visitors and newcomers remark, with surprise, on the friendliness and helpfulness they experience. Members exchange and give away produce and there are always offers of assistance. Peter added that most plots are worked organically these days and with pleasure he has seen the arrival of buzzards, sparrow hawks and even red kites.

An interesting dig

71. Peter's allotment finds - pottery and bottle shards. Photo with kind permission of John Connolly.

72. Bottles unearthed when the digger removed the bank. Photo with kind permission of John Connolly.

Peter Norris, who has three plots around the community area, is a keen amateur archaeologist particularly when it comes to digging his allotments. Over the years he has unearthed numerous shards of glass and pottery, along with complete bottles. He admits to having a degree in cultural and historical studies and that finding such material is a bit of a passion. Due to Clarence Road being fairly central to the town, with footpaths going through the allotment site in the past, plus road sweepings being deposited on it, it is perhaps not surprising that so much evidence of the past can still be found. Bottles unearthed by the digger on the bank show that allotmenteering was thirsty work. There was ginger beer by R Fry & Co on the south coast, and shandy from Maidstone in Kent. Not forgetting man's best friend, a bottle of Benbow's Dog Mixture was also found, which was meant to purify the blood and produce smooth shiny coats. Nothing of great value but a great window into the everyday past.

Clarence Road allotment site today

As with any allotment site a band of volunteers are relied upon for essential maintenance such as hedge trimming and ditch clearing. There is the occasional working party but these are not regular. The Clarence Road site is certainly a breath of fresh air in the town, surrounded as it is with houses and roads. There seem to be lots of greenhouses and a profusion of flowers being grown among the vegetables, consequently it attracts lots of wildlife and pollinators.

In early Spring this year, 2022, Richard Evans took on a small plot having been on the waiting list a little while. He told me what it was like obtaining a small plot on Clarence Road site. Richard wrote:

'We were given a great welcome by our fellow allotment holders, who were keen to encourage our initial endeavours and give advice about what had done well in the plot before we took it on. There is great generosity at the allotment with plot holders swapping or giving away plants and produce. When we first started, we were given strawberry plants that were going spare by a plot neighbour and my son Woody and my two-year-old niece set about planting them, and a couple of months later, took great pride in eating them!

73. David Hide and Carol Hayton's plot.

'There is a strong community at the site, be it wise-heads who have worked the land for years or new enthusiasts who are in a similar position to us. I have two children, Ella, nine, and Woody, five, and both love having an allotment at Clarence Road. Several of their friends are also plot holders – they are always delighted to see each other and it's a wonderful place for them to explore and learn together.

'It has been great for the kids to learn where fresh produce comes from and as a family, our eyes have been opened as to the time and care that goes in to creating the fruit and vegetables, we often take for granted. We certainly waste less food now and having a compost bin is helping us to recycle even more. With the help of friends, family and fellow plot holders we have had a bountiful first summer and enjoyed many a tomato and courgette! We hope to have many more years at the plot and hope to inspire the next generation to grow their own too.'

Richard's impressions on taking on an allotment for the first time, and the benefits and enjoyment his family get from it is lovely to hear and sums up what many of us feel about our allotments.

Bob

Plot Holder for 12 years

Ann & Ian

Plot Holders for 18 years

Cathie

Plot Holder for 10 years

Özgür

Plot Holder for 2 years

Richard & Woody

Plot Holders for 6 months

Greg & Alice

Plot Holders for 4 years

Donna

Plot Holder for 18 months

Nicola

Plot Holder for 5 years

Drew

Plot Holder for 3 years

Pete

Plot Holder for 31 years

Lesley

Plot Holder for 4 years

Joseph

Plot Holder for 6 months

74. Some of the Clarence Road allotment site plot holders, old and new, working on their plots and proud of them, as they should be. Photo with kind permission of John Connolly, 2022.

Spring on the Plot

I rest from digging, stretch and listen to
a woodpecker drilling the distant oak,
still cold air vibrating with sudden sound.

I smile, nature is beginning to move,
daffodils bunched and bent from recent winds,
pale primroses peeping from grassy banks.

A solitary bee, up too early,
unstable on stiff winter wings, zig-zags
across the plot, befuddled and buzzing.

I bend to plant plugs of broad bean seedlings,
their long white roots bursting with energy,
tops unfurling tight hooks of new green leaves.

I think of April and my spirits rise,
warmer days, longer light, lockdown loosening.

Chapter 9: *Depot Road Allotments*

75. One of the three entrance gates to Depot Road allotments off Depot Road.

Depot Road Allotments site is one of the larger Horsham town sites of about four acres (1.6 ha) with about 120 plots. Many of the ten rod (16 ft, 4.8 m) plots are divided into smaller sizes. Since 2013, the management of the site is by Depot Road Allotment Society, a committee of volunteers, Bob Essex is the current Chairman and Caroline Cann the Treasurer.

I talked to Bob Essex in summer 2021 and he told me they are careful to check that new plot holders are managing and they keep an eye on plots that are not being worked and are overrun with weeds. They do not often ask people to leave but have done so when really necessary.

On taking on a plot there is a refundable deposit that pays

76. Another of the three entrance gates to Depot Road Allotments off Depot Road.

for any strimming and maintenance of a weedy plot before new people take it on. One generous plot holder cuts all the grass paths on the site, although it is actually the responsibility of each plot holder to cut their own paths. Likewise, if anyone is ill or in hospital, volunteers will try and help by watering, strimming or covering a plot until the plot holder can return to look after it.

In 2017, before the pandemic, as noted in an article about the allotment site in All About Horsham (AAH) magazine, there were actually about nine free plots, but during the pandemic the waiting list rose to over forty.

77. Chairman, Bob Essex by his allotment.

There appears to be a very good community spirit on the Depot Road site. In the centre of the allotments is a large hut, set in a wood chipped space with seating and a table for exchanging surplus plants, vegetables and fruit. There is a coffee morning here every second Sunday of the month, cakes are brought and hot drinks laid on. Donations are encouraged for an annual charity, and a number of allotment themed competitions, such as the most bee friendly plot, or the most unusual vegetable grown. In 2021, this prize went to Peter Boardman for growing the somewhat exotic Achocha, which is a relative of the courgette from the high Andes and can be fried or baked. Inside the community hut are kept tools like a mower and strimmer that plot holders can borrow on arrangement.

78. The community area with shed.

A very informative newsletter is prepared by a volunteer and sent out each season. It covers a variety of helpful information such as jobs for the month, planting by the moon, ways to save water, updates on the bees, news of plot holders, and, of course, the yearly competitions.

In 2022 there will be a return of the popular and fun Vegetable and Fruit Show which judges produce under three categories: most unusual shape, most unusual type, and most unusual size. With a 2021 competition for bee friendly plots, it is perhaps unsurprising that on one of the plots, under a tree near the top of the hill, are beehives kept by an experienced beekeeper.

79. The beehive plot.

There appears to be quite a good cross-section of community at these allotments. There are as many women plot holders as men, but also couples and families. Most ages are represented, in addition to Eastern European and Asian families. Before the pandemic two plots were assigned to two different charities. These were the Strawford Centre, Blatchford Close, Horsham, a learning disability day centre. The other plot was used by the Richmond Fellowship, based in Park Street, who assist people with mental health and wellbeing. Knowing how much working with nature in the peace and quiet of an allotment can assist our physical and mental wellbeing it is a shame, but understandable, that these organisations were no longer able to support their plots on the Depot Road site.

80. One of several bee friendly plots on the site.

The site has three gates onto Depot Road, and three green tracks running up the site which is on a hill. This has implications for flooding, as in winter the lower allotments near the road can be flooded up to a foot deep. One plot holder,

81. Andrew Layzell working on his plot.

Andrew Layzell, whose plot is in this area, is in the process of moving plots. Although his wildflower area, sown by his wife, Julia, and which won the most bee friendly plot competition in 2021, will stay. The plot next to him in this damp area is also gardened for wildlife by Lucy Cotter who has a small pond and lots of rough places for slow worms and other species to enjoy. By each gate and halfway up the hill by each green track is a tap and a large container or tank. Hosepipes are forbidden. There appear to be quite a few structures on the site, sheds, greenhouses and polytunnels, none of them big. Permission has to be sought to erect anything and consideration given to size and the effect on other nearby plot holders, but clearly permission is usually given.

From the archives

According to the 1840 Tithe Map, the area where the Depot Road Allotment site is now, used to be arable fields belonging to Grub Street and Depot Farms both owned by Robert Hurst and occupied by tenant farmer Richard Howes. In the council archives the first mention of allotments on Depot Road is in a letter from the council in February 1917, referring to an application for an allotment to grow potatoes and other vegetables. The only land available was grassland on the south side of Depot Road belonging to Herbert Agate who was willing to provide ten allotments of about nine rods each. Interestingly, one of these plots was let to the Women's Social and Literary Club based at 60 West Street, Horsham.

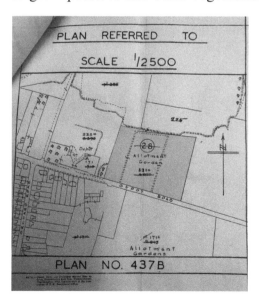

82. Plan from the sale document 24.4.1950 between the Hurst estate and Horsham Urban District Council. WSRO UD/ HO/21/2/249.

In 1938, King & Chasemore alerted the Council to the sale of Depot Farm, forty acres suitable for building and, '… close to the famous St Leonard's Forest.', with the station not far away and with the added attraction that the trains would be electrified on 3rd July 1938. The land was bounded by Kings Road and Crawley Road to the north and Depot Road to the south. More of the Hurst Park estate was sold after the death of Arthur Reginald Hurst in March 1948. Land in Depot Road, both on the north and south side came up for auction but were initially unsold. Roffey and District Allotment Society were interested but withdrew due to the cost quoted of £500. Eventually, the north side of four acres with a frontage of 480 ft onto Depot Road, was bought by the council on 24th April 1950, for £400.

In providing information to the district valuer in January 1948, it was noted that this land was already let to various allotment holders providing a rent of £14 9s 3d per annum presumably to the Hurst Estates. There is mention of fifty-four plots of mostly ten rods with six being half size and sixteen between seven and nine rods.

This land had been zoned under the council Planning Scheme for permanent allotments. The south side of Depot Road was of course zoned for a school building.

Remembering the past

According to Sylvia Murrell, an ex-plot holder, now in her mid-eighties, a long-standing member of the committee, the allotment rules used to be much stricter. She remembers her husband being told off just for putting pulled weeds on the path. She and her husband got their first plot in 1963. At that time there was no water laid onto the site and she remembered her husband had to fill watering cans and wheelbarrow them from home up to the plot. They had two plots, mostly vegetables and a young family, so she was very busy. She does, however, remember lovely picnics on the plot. They moved plots to the top of the hill, cutting down the size of the plots and with a proper greenhouse in which they grew tomatoes.

83. Sylvia Murrell on her plot in 2021, she has since retired from her allotment.

When I spoke to her on her plot in summer 2021, her butternut squash looked brilliant but she was not quite sure how long she could continue the demands of an allotment. Her husband Mick had passed on and her children were no longer at home, but she enjoyed the social side, as well as the pleasures of growing. She thought it might be her last year as an active plot holder and that has proved correct. She gave up her plot in spring 2022.

In the Depot Road Allotment Society newsletter, spring 2022 they had a feature on memories of the allotments. One contributor, Bryan Wicks, wrote as follows:

84. Depot Road Allotments in the 1970s. Image copyright © Ray Luff, Horsham Museum.

'My father took on his allotment at Depot Road Allotments in 1958 which was thirteen rods at the rear left of the allotment. Most plot holders had similar sized plots and all plots were open ground. Raised beds are a more recent addition to allotments. I initially helped him on his plot and then took on my own plot later. There was no water available at the allotment in those days and the houses in Corunna Drive helped plot holders by filling baths on the allotment with water from their houses using a hosepipe. Also, the chimney sweep used to tip soot just inside the first gate for plot holders to use, as it was particularly good for growing celery.

'Most plot holders were men and traditional English veg was grown on plots. No courgettes were seen growing in those days! There were also very strict rules about erecting a shed or greenhouse and permission had to be granted by the

council. However, the shed that is still in the far-left hand corner of the allotment, is the one built by me and my father in the 1960s. There used to be a brickworks at the back of the allotment, where Pollards Drive is now, and there were remnants of the observer place in the far-right hand corner of the allotment, as used by the Royal Observer Corp in World War II.

'Initially plot holders were concerned that the allotments were a temporary arrangement but in the 1960s, the Treasurer of Horsham Urban District Council had a house in Pollards Drive and plot holders were relieved when he took on an allotment, as they felt the allotments were now here to stay!'

What our allotment means to us

During the Covid pandemic the society became aware of how beneficial the allotment plots were to people and so gathered some anonymous comments asking members what their allotment meant to them, here a some of those comments:

'Watching miracles occur as a small seed grows into a delicious vegetable.'

'Enjoying vegetables that taste far better than anything you can buy in a supermarket.'

'A solution to many of life's problems by providing a haven of calm to help my mental well-being and keep me fit with natural doses of Vitamin D3 from the sunshine.'

'An introduction to new friends who can share experience and tips for growing fruit and veg or for just having a socially distanced chat with in these troubled, challenging times.'

'The allotment has always been a place for me to escape to and spend a couple of hours trying to forget some of life's problems.

'Since lockdown it has become much more than that. The allotment has become a refuge and once through the gate you know you are safe and for the next couple of hours the rest of world doesn't exist. It has helped me keep my sanity.

'On a lighter note, the extra time spent down there has enabled me to try out new vegetable varieties like the black forest courgette and blue banana squash, both of which are doing very well.'

'My allotment has meant everything to me. I was working directly with families affected by Covid-19 deaths and the allotment has been my place to escape during lockdown when there was nowhere else to go. I don't know what I would've done without it. It's also my first year having a plot, and now I can't imagine what I did with all my time before it. A little slice of heaven.'

85. View of allotment plots at Depot Road allotments, 'A little slice of heaven.'

Painting 7. Beetroot, by Dr Maggie Weir-Wilson

Chapter 10: *Harwood Road Allotments*

86. Entrance to Harwood Road Allotments from Harwood Road.

Harwood Road Allotments site comes under the management of North Horsham Parish Council, but it also has an association made up of six volunteers, three with positions of Chairman, Secretary and Treasurer. I was able to discuss the site with the Chair, John Commins. Few archives or paperwork appeared to be available in the West Sussex Records Office, or Horsham Museum, however North Horsham Parish Council did provide the front page and map of the original lease which was very helpful.

It is a small site of about 1.5 acres (0.6 ha) immediately bordering Harwood Road. Due to the large grass verge, there is no easy access for deliveries of such things as manure or chippings. It has two small entrances, both

87. Wide verge along Harwood Road with allotments, hedge on the left and road beyond the grass on the right.

gated and locked. There are about twenty-six plots, mostly about eight rods in size with many split into a half or quarter. The site lost about eight plots when the nearby housing development, Manor Fields, was built at the western end in the 1980s.

88. Chairman, John Commins on his allotment plot growing sweetcorn.

Due to the small size of the site, there is no toilet or community area or building. Also, there are no bonfire sites or wildlife plots. Water was laid on about twenty years ago and they now have six taps but sprinklers and hoses are not allowed. There are few structures on the site and sheds have to be of a reasonable size for the plot. As on most allotment sites volunteers maintain the grass and hedges. The school on the northern boundary, Leechpool Primary School, requested a half plot and they were given this near an entrance to their school playing grounds.

There appears to have been some wrangling between the parish council and the committee about responsibilities over the years, such as who cares for the row of large oak trees and ditch on the northern boundary between the school and the allotment site. The tall wire fencing to the south which borders the road has also been under dispute. On the plus side there is little vandalism or theft, just damage from pigeons. Also, the fencing keeps out the deer who used to come over from the forest to see what they could munch. This was very common twenty odd years ago before the fencing was installed.

From the archives

North Horsham Parish Council has in their possession a copy of the original lease dated 28th June 1978. This is a contract between West Sussex County Council and Horsham Rural Parish Council for the tenancy of said land of 1.4 acres (0.56 ha) for five years at an initial payment of £150 and then 5p a year payable on the 1st January each year. There are some reservations in favour of the County Council with regard to mineral rights, timber and trees, game and hunting.

There clearly must have been demand for allotments in the 70s as at a similar time the Roffey Allotment site off Beech Road was set up, according to Janis Maynard whose parents lived in Beech Road around that time.

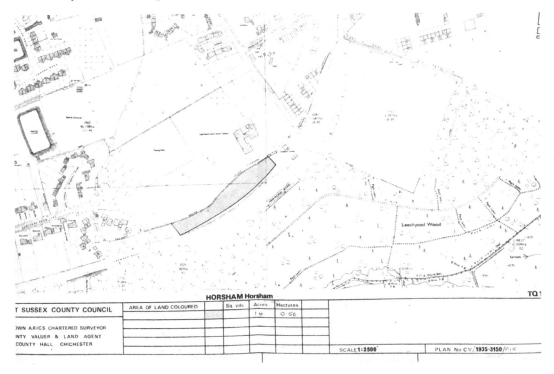

89. Map attached to the 1978 lease, showing allotment land in pink. With kind permission of North Horsham Parish Council.

Remembering the past

I was very grateful to Janis Maynard who grew up near Leechpool in the 1950s and 60s and was able to share some memories from that time. She remembered that the land where the allotments are now, was originally a field at the back of Leechpool Farm Cottage which reached as far as the tree line of Leechpool Woods. She knew the family that lived in the cottage and told me that she used to play with their children on this field, which apparently housed an old wooden shed and lots of feral cats. Leechpool Farm itself amounted to forty-three acres of arable and pastureland which was owned by the Hurst family. Much of the land around Roffey, owned by the Hurst's, was sold in 1911 but this farm did not reach its reserve price. It continued as a tenanted poultry farm.

I had wondered whether the allotment land was from the Harwood House estate, a large mansion and parkland which lay off the Kings Road, owned by the Lyons family, and latterly by the two single Lyons sisters who devoted their time to running a fine stable of thoroughbred horses.

Once the sisters had died, the council acquired the estate and the house was demolished around 1965. Harwood Road was built through the gardens and on through Leechpool Farm. Janis Maynard remembered practicing three-point turns with her father on the unopened road in 1969. In 1970 it was opened as a Roffey relief road. This of course opened up the area for housing development and the building of Leechpool Primary School.

90. Leechpool Primary School pupils working on their allotment plots on Harwood Road. With kind permission of Leechpool Primary School.

Leechpool Primary School

I asked Nicola Davenport, Head of Leechpool Primary School about the school taking on an allotment plot on the Harwood Road Allotment site, the experiences and learning the children were benefitting from. She told me the following,

'The children had been developing their allotment in Harwood Road for nearly two years, and it has been a wonderful project for the children to get involved with. They have enjoyed working in the community, developing a fruit, vegetable,

116

flower and herb garden. The success of each has varied but the children have not been deterred and have even enjoyed harvesting the produce from the allotment. This has resulted in some very tasty meals being cooked and shared.

91. General view of the Harwood Road Allotments site towards the school boundary.

'The children have enjoyed the opportunity to design posters to illustrate the growing areas, dig and cultivate the areas, weed and water the different plants as they grow. They have learnt about the need to water the produce and to ensure that a regular eye is kept on the produce especially in the very hot days we have enjoyed this summer.

'All the children are excited to be involved, from the Nursery class to Year 6 who will be heading off to secondary education at the end of the year. The leadership of the project was initially taken on by one of the science teachers but now we have a full-time lead, Alice Mcilwraith, who coordinates the Allotment Project. She would say that gardening wasn't her thing but over the months, working with the children and classes she has enjoyed the project and the amazing outcomes from the allotment. As a school, we still have a long way to go to ensure we make use of the space throughout the year but we are keen to learn. We have resilience and determination. We have also had a great deal of success although some of this can be attributed to the many friends we have made with our neighbouring allotment enthusiasts.

'The time at the allotment is enjoyed by all and our knowledge of plants, vegetables and herbs has increased no end. We are also very keen tasters of the produce we grow and we are starting to organise our allotment to ensure it can be as productive as possible throughout the year. Going forward we will look to selling our produce and using it to develop mathematical skills of weighing and measuring. We think the opportunities for learning from the allotment are going to be endless. We are always looking for suggestions, so any ideas please send them our way!'

92. General view of the Harwood Road Allotments site towards the school boundary.

It is great to hear such a positive endorsement for getting young children involved in growing and noticing nature. One hopes more of Horsham's allotment sites might consider linking up with local schools. The results are great for future generations of community, allotments sites and production of food.

Harwood Road allotment site today

There is some diversity on the site, growers include Portuguese, Iraqi, Chinese and two Syrian refugees who share a plot. The Leechpool Primary School is on the northern border and they have a gate onto the allotments from the school grounds. There does not appear to be any regular allotment gatherings, perhaps because it is a small site. As with all Horsham allotments at this current time there is a waiting list.

Hills Cemetery

Ashes to ashes, dust to dust,
allotments to cemetery.

Soil, a bond between life and death.
Its myriad mycorrhiza filaments
communicating complex messages.

Microorganisms releasing nutrients,
sustaining life; dealing with death and decay.
Worms, woodlice, ants and tiny insects
pitching in, the ultimate recyclers

The allotments were only temporary,
plot holders dug, tilled and weeded,
planted out seedlings with pride. Neat rows
of beans, lettuces and cabbages.

Quietly, beyond the hedge, the stone rows
of graves, freshly dug, moving closer,
the cemetery waiting to claim this rich soil.

Ashes to ashes, dust to dust,
allotments to cemetery.

Chapter 11: Hills Farm Allotments

HILLS FARM
ALLOTMENT ASSOCIATION
◆
THIS IS A PRIVATE AREA
NO TRESPASSERS
NO PUBLIC RIGHT OF WAY

HILLS FARM
ALLOTMENT ASSOCIATION
◆
PLEASE REMEMBER IF YOU
ARE THE LAST LEAVING THE
ALLOTMENT SITE YOU
MUST CLOSE THE GATES.
The Committee

93. Entrance gate to the allotment section of Hills Cemetery.

The land on which Hills Cemetery and the last vestiges of the Hills Farm Allotments are situated on what was originally Hills Farm, part of the 200-acre (80 ha) Hills estate owned by the 9th Viscount Irwin of Temple Newsam in Leeds, and his wife Frances Shepheard who had inherited Hills through her family. Although this wealthy couple spent most of their time in Temple Newsam, they came once a year to Hills where Frances involved herself in the politics ensuring her candidate became MP. In the 1760s, the Irwin's employed Lancelot 'Capability' Brown to redesign the Hills parkland, altering the River Arun into serpentine lakes, planting trees and making eye-catching features. Viscount Irwin died in 1778 and Frances remained committed to Hills until her death in 1807. Her son-in-law inherited and promptly sold the estate, at a good price, to the Duke of Norfolk who was after the political influence vested in it. He was not interested in the house or lovely garden so the mansion was pulled down and in 1820 the park was sold off, the lakes filled in and it was returned to agriculture.

94. Path to the allotment section of Hills Cemetery.

95. Poster issued in April 1937 by Horsham Urban District Council advertising for tenants to take temporary allotments on Hills Cemetery site. Horsham Museum and Art Gallery.

The Denne Road Cemetery was opened for burials in July 1852, after St Mary's graveyard became full. Denne Road Cemetery was extended in 1881 but it also was becoming increasingly full by the end of the century. So, in 1900, fifteen acres of Hills Farm was purchased by Horsham Urban and Rural District Councils for a new town cemetery and it was opened two years later. As can be seen in the poster illustrated below, the Horsham Burial District Joint Committee invited tenants to take-up allotment plots within the cemetery on a temporary basis in April 1937 and from the wording it would appear that this was already an ongoing arrangement.

Hills Cemetery was increased in size in 1923 and then again in 1956. The southern top section was given over to temporary allotments until such time as they were needed for burials. Since then, demand has continued to increase and in 2004 ten plots were taken by the cemetery. At this time the Hills Farm Allotment Society which manage the site was advised that it would be another twelve to fifteen years before any more plots were taken. However, in November 2007, Horsham District Council agreed to extend the cemetery into the total adjoining allotment space within the next ten years, when it expected the land would be needed for more burials. The Argus newspaper reported some consternation over this amongst existing plot holders who had spent money on their allotments, and the Chairs of both Hills Farm and Shelley allotments had reported greater demand for allotments, both sites having waiting lists. Today there are about ten remaining plots, and these are expected to go in the next few years.

96. Hills Cemetery.

97. Some of the few allotments now left on Hills Farm Cemetery land.

Painting 8. Chillies, by Dr Maggie Weir-Wilson

Chapter 12: *Lower Barn Close Allotments*

98. Entrance gate to site.

At the end of Lower Barn Close cul- de-sac, which is off the Rusper Road, is the entrance to the Lower Barn Close allotments. There is very little parking available outside the site, perhaps two cars, and a rather anonymous looking gate. One cannot see into the allotments until you go through the gate, which is kept locked.

The site is roughly triangular and about two acres. It is bounded on one side by the railway line and platforms of Littlehaven Station, and on the other side by housing. Mary Yeoman had heard that it used to be a much larger site with the allotments going as far as the Rusper Road but social housing was built over most of it in the 1940s. There are four allotments still existing from this time, which are situated

99. Allotments beyond the entrance gate.

behind four houses on Lower Barn Close and rented by those residents. These are not for rent publicly and are not part of the Lower Barn Allotment Society. On the main site there are currently forty-three plot holders on forty-six plots of varying size and, of course, a waiting list.

100. Western boundary of site up against the railway and platforms.

101. The community container or shed.

Maintenance of grass paths and hedges relies on volunteers with the time, energy and equipment to undertake such tasks. Near the entrance is a large metal container which is used as a community shed and contains useful equipment owned by the society, which can be used by plot holders with committee permission.

Although people did tell me it was a friendly site and much appreciated during the recent pandemic lockdown, there are no community events as such. There is no toilet facility. Water is available through four taps, one with a tank, and hose pipes are not allowed. Water recovery is encouraged on structures.

There are no set-aside wildlife plots as such, but the site is known to have foxes and slow worms. Mary Yeoman told me that her son-in-law kept bees for a while behind high fences on a plot, but about four years ago someone got stung and there were worries that the bees were rather close to other plot holders and neighbours, so that was the end of beekeeping on the allotments.

From the archives

The 1840 Tithe Map shows the area of Lower Barn Close allotments as part of Parsonage or Parsons Farm owned by Robert Hurst and rented by John Peters, senior, at that time. By 1939 London Passenger Transport Group appears to have purchased eight acres of this farm and it was noted that the area between Kings Road and Parsonage Road, to the south of Lower Barn Close, were being used as allotments, about eighty plots. These particular allotments have since disappeared under housing.

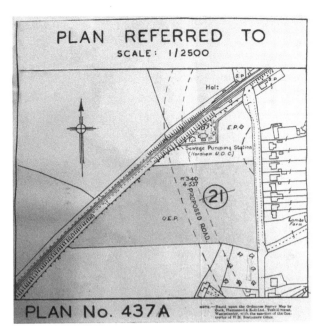

102. Plan 437A of purchased land by HUDC and subsequent Lower Barn Close Allotments.

However, in 1948, on the death of Arthur Reginald Hurst, the Hurst Park estate was sold and the council bought four acres, two rods and six poles, for £450. From the plan 437A attached to the sales details dated 24th April 1950, this is

clearly where Lower Barn Close allotments were to be situated, between the Rusper Road and the railway, but perhaps, as suggested by Mary Yeoman, they originally occupied this whole stretch? The proposed road outlined on the plan did not go ahead but smaller roads such as Lower Barn Close were built along with housing, with a remaining two acres left for allotments.

Plot holder Francis Vernon pointed me in the direction of an OS map 25-inch 1892-1914 digitised by the National Library of Scotland which clearly shows a small block of *allotment gardens* exactly at the site, but not as large as the area shown pink in Plan 437A. This means that the allotments were certainly older than 1948.

103. Francis Vernon clearing pumpkins from his plot in 2021.

127

Remembering the past

Francis was also able to talk to an older plot holder, Dennis, who was born on the nearby Wimblehurst Farm in 1939. He remembers that there were always some allotments on the current site in his childhood. Lower Barn Close did not exist then, and the fields went up to Rusper Road, by Littlehaven Station. Dennis's grandfather and uncle worked on the farm, which had some cows that produced milk for the local delivery company, possibly called Standings? There was also market gardening where there are now flats at the north end of Wimblehurst Road. A reminder of how rural the edges of Horsham were eighty years ago.

A more recent memory was told to me by Mary Yeoman. Her daughter and son-in-law had started to rent two allotment plots in about 2005, and she came to help them in 2013. At that time there were sheds and various structures on most plots. However, the rules on sheds required plot holders to ask permission. She said there are stories of a particular shed being rather popular, its owner being fond of a tipple and the shed seeming an ideal place for a bar.

104. Trevor and Shirley Lillywhite.

The longest plot holders on the site have got to be Trevor and Shirley Lillywhite who manage a seven rod site near the entrance. When I visited in early autumn 2021, they were clearing and digging a section in preparation for winter. They have been on the Lower Barn site for forty-two years but moved from a far corner to be nearer the entrance, aware that it was less far to carry things. There is not much room for cars or deliveries throughout the site, but it is possible to get in through the gate and park there.

The Inventive Allotmenteers

Plot holder Nero Gilissen, is particularly inventive and is building a solar panel driven irrigation system from his shed to a geodesic dome greenhouse. He has established a wormery for composting and intends to garden biodynamically, which is another interesting departure for allotments.

The allotment holders on Lower Barn are not only inventive, but alert to the possibilities of recycling. One person started growing carrots in an old bath, and another has followed his example. It seems a good tip if one can get the bath onto the site. On one plot there are three! The carrots remain far enough above the ground to avoid carrot fly and yet the soil in the bath is deep enough to produce good carrots. Other root crops like parsnips could be grown like this as well. In addition to old baths, old wooden crates are also used.

106. Nero Gilissen's geodesic dome greenhouse.

105. Nero Gilissen with his irrigation system.

107. Carrots growing in a bath on one of the plots.

Lower Barn Close allotment site today

As with other town allotments there is a long waiting list for plots on this site, but new members are always welcomed when a plot comes available. There are working parties of volunteer plot holders who continue to carry out the bigger jobs on site such as the recent removal of a tree and dealing with brambles along the railway fence.

More plot holders are growing flowers these days as a *crop* and picking them for home or family weddings, so much cheaper than bought flowers, fresher and less air miles.

The committee are interested in promoting stronger links with the community around them and so will be hoping to establish this in the coming years.

108. Sweet peas going home by bike. Photo with kind permission of Francis Vernon.

Painting 9. Artichokes, by Dr Maggie Weir-Wilson

Chapter 13: *Roffey Allotments*

109. The main entrance gate in 2021, now a metal gate and adjacent to a large playing field.

This allotment site is about 2.5 acres (1 ha) on the north-east edge of Horsham between a recreation ground and Newhouse Farm. I visited in late September 2021 and spoke to Ian Penfold, the retiring Plot Secretary of Roffey Allotment Society. The Plot Secretary is responsible for letting vacant plots and ensuring the site and infrastructure is maintained appropriately.

Ian was able to tell me that originally, the plots were mostly ten rods, but today they are differing sizes such as five rods and even 2.5, mini plots. There are about sixty-one plot holders and a waiting list. Whereas in the past it was mainly men taking on the plots, today over 40 per cent are women and there are many on the waiting list. There is an ethnic diversity from Italian, to German and Eastern European. As can be seen from the photos there is a lot of grass, and a lot of hedging to keep trimmed. The grass cutting is done by a group of about

110. Boundary hedge and grass tracks that all need maintenance by volunteers.

111. Boundary hedge and grass tracks that all need maintenance by volunteers.

112. One of the two community sheds.

113. Heather Playfoot's dahlias and shed.

five volunteers who have mowers and there is an annual hedge cutting weekend where plot holders are encouraged to volunteer to help with cutting the hedges.

There are two community sheds on the site. One, just off the main grass track up from the gate is an old railway shed. Tools and such like are kept in them for general use but must be returned. The second one is an old shed on a plot surrounded by trees and hedges at the far end of the site backing onto Beech Road. Barbeque equipment is also in this shed. Before the pandemic, community barbeques used to be held and probably will be again.

There are three tanks of water with two taps each, one for a hose to be attached – unlike many other allotment sites – and the other tap to fill the tank. There is no toilet or shop but there is a seed scheme, due to the Roffey Allotment Society being a member of the National Allotment and Leisure Gardens Association. Kings Seeds catalogues are kept in the community sheds for plot holders to take part in the seed scheme. The rules on sheds and structures are laxer than they used to be and many plot holders now have sheds, small polytunnels and greenhouses. They do have to ask permission and this is usually granted. Ian said that bonfires became a bone of contention a few years ago. Plot holders used to be allowed to have their own bonfires, but due to complaints and concerns about insurance liability, there is now just one annual communal bonfire. Other options for dealing with burnable waste are being considered.

Roffey Allotment Society has always been a self-managed society since it was set up in 1983, renting the land from the council. However, unlike other Horsham allotment sites, it opted to become a cooperative organisation when the lease came up for renewal in 2017. Dave Chambers, the current Treasurer, explained to me that the problem was lack of volunteers to become trustees and thus take liability for the site. However, in a co-operative all the plot holders are shareholders and thus liability is shared. There is some advantage to having a corporate identity and there are other allotment sites in the country on the co-op register. They have to abide by co-operative guidelines and if a plot is being neglected then the plot holder can only be removed through a vote at the AGM, rather than the usual warnings followed by eviction.

114. The wildlife plot 2021 with half hidden bug hotel.

One rather nice feature in a plot near the entrance and the playing field is a wildlife haven. This is overseen by Ian Penfold and was full of nasturtium, cosmos and other flowering plants when I visited. In the centre is a bug hotel, almost overwhelmed by wildflowers and grasses. I visited again in 2022 and could see the bug house a bit more clearly.

115. The wildlife plot 2022 with a more clearly visible bug hotel.

As with most modern plots, flowers are a particular pleasure to grow and pick. Ian has grown dahlias on his since the beginning. I also spoke to Heather Playfoot who explained that she had originally grown dahlias for her daughter's wedding, which was continually postponed over the pandemic, however she now has a wonderful plot full of dahlias. She has also recently acquired a shed made by her engineer dad from old pallets. Good recycling. Another impressive plot is number 20b worked by Janis Ford, who produces a lovely display of flowers.

116. Janis Ford's plot full of flowers. dahlias and shed.

From the archives

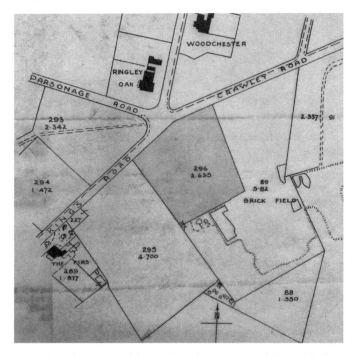

The 1840 Tithe Map, shows an allotment site off the Crawley Road to the west of the Horsham Union Workhouse, one of three Horsham Labourers Friend Society sites, this one was rented from Robert Hurst. According to the Labourers Friend audit, this site had eight plots and was called the Star. Archives are then limited until the 1930s and 40s. At this time the Roffey and District Allotment Society was looking for more allotment land and approached the Canadian Military, as they were

117. Plan showing field 296 for sale. Later used for Redkiln Way. HMRO MS UD/HO/21/2/67.

occupying the workhouse and base hospital, suggesting that any allotments could be returned to them when needed. However, they were knocked back by the Canadians who felt that the area of garden should be retained and cultivated for the purpose of garden supplies for the hospital personnel and patients. In April 1942, the Roffey and District Allotment Society wrote to the council regretting that land was so difficult to obtain for allotments.

At this time, they again approached the council and raised the proposition for the purchase of field 296 (see map above) which was up for sale. It was 2.6 acres (1 ha) which was criticised locally for being used for pony riding rather than food production. The society also suggested that the council buy six acres of land at the back of Roffey Post Office on the Crawley Road. However once the owners were found, it was felt to be too expensive.

In the late 1930s the council also approached the Lyons sisters of Harwood House to see if they would sell some meadow adjoining Kings Road for permanent allotments. This also came to nothing. Another attempt by Roffey and District

Society was to suggest to the council that south of Depot Road could be used but they were told that this was reserved under the town planning scheme for a school, which eventually was Forest Girls School, renamed Millais School in 1976.

There is nothing more in the archives but clearly Roffey Allotment Society found land available in Honeysuckle Walk, as people remember the old allotments there, before they moved to Beech Road.

Remembering the past

In talking to Ian Penfold, he was clear that the Roffey allotments were only moved quite recently to their present site. Originally, possibly after the Second World War, they were situated where Honeysuckle Walk is now, off Lambs Farm Road and near the playing field. However, in the mid-1980s the council wanted to sell this land for building and so with considerable persuasion from the allotment committee an alternative was offered. A field of about 2.5 acres was bought by Horsham District Council from the builders Wimpey who were at that time developing Beech Road. The area was fenced and gated and leased

118. Ian Penfold and his allotment in 2021.

to the allotment holders for them to mark it out and create the allotments. Ian Penfold first had his plot in 1987 and remembers the difficult soil, hard clay and iron stone, but he says it has improved over the years as it was cultivated. He moved to a different plot, nearer the main gate, where he is today.

The current Roffey Allotments Society was founded in 1983 by John Cherriman, who became its first secretary, in addition to doing other tasks like practical site maintenance. When he passed away on 26th May 2020, in his mid-eighties, Roffey plot holders produced an appreciation of all the work he had done, plus memories, which his family have kindly shared with me. It is a testament to his determination and enthusiasm for allotmenteering that he initially negotiated with the council to get the site designated as allotments and he agreed and signed the original lease. He then prepared the site by organising the installation of water, fences and gates, and marking out the plots, much of this done by himself with any volunteers he could recruit.

A number of long-standing plot holders remembered him fondly.

119. John Cherriman, Founder of the Roffey Allotment Society. Photo with kind permission of the Roffey Allotment Society.

Christina Harrison wrote, 'He was very instrumental in helping me set up as a complete novice. I would often pop by his plot to borrow equipment in the nearby communal shed before I had any of my own tools and would end up chatting and receiving much appreciated advice and tips. His compost system was second to none, very organised with a three-year system going on.'

Stella Eve noted, 'John Cherriman was my first point of contact with Roffey Allotments and from that first meeting, till we left to move away, I always admired his gentle, no-nonsense relationship with vegetable growing. His knowledge came from a lifetime of practical experience and his plot was a joy to behold.'

However, like many of the older allotmenteers he was a bit dubious about women plot holders. Some remember being given a plot on the edge of the site, under trees and far away from the water tap, other women got the same treatment. But it seems he grew to respect women gardeners. Heather Salter-Smith was on the plot next to him for twenty-five years and found him always helpful in passing on advice. Plot-holder Peter Batchelor was most impressed with the amount he did for the Society, being secretary, initially running the seed purchase scheme and mowing all the main paths for many years.

I was able to talk to Heather Salter-Smith about other memories of the site since she had her plot for about thirty years. She was on the committee for twenty years and had run the seed purchase scheme through the National Society of Allotment and Leisure Gardens (NSALG) for five years. Heather had to stand down from the committee when she became the auditor for the society's cooperative accounts. She remembers Ian winning gold three times for his best allotment when Horsham in Bloom were running those competitions. She grows the usual fruit and vegetables, although less brassicas than when she first started. She recommended using beetroot for a chocolate beetroot cake (see below) which sounded delicious. Flowers are a new thing for her in the last three or four years, and she grew dahlias for the first-time last year. She usually grows sweet peas as they are reliable, and she has sunflowers which tend to self-seed. When they are over, the sunflower heads go to a friend for her chickens to peck at.

120. Heather Salter-Smith on her plot.

When thinking about the site more generally, Heather remembered the threat of building in the next field but following considerable opposition and the fact that it fell within a site of outstanding natural beauty this plan was rejected. The maintenance of boundaries has caused problems over the years, one side being the responsibility of neighbouring householders and the other three maintained by the allotments, including a native hedge planted by them. There is a low metal gate provided by the council and not worth locking.

Thankfully, there has not been much trouble over the years, just some teenagers smoking dope and one naughty woman taking produce. Both were challenged. Bonfires have caused the usual problems with neighbours and now they ae not allowed except for a community bonfire once a year on a vacant plot. Before the pandemic there was an annual barbeque but this was abandoned in the pandemic and has not restarted.

A recipe: Heather's Chocolate Beetroot Cake

Ingredients:

    6oz/175g Plain Flour

    2oz/50g Cocoa Powder

    1.5 tsp Baking Powder

    7oz/200g Caster Sugar

    9oz/250g Cooked Beetroot

    7floz/200ml Sunflower Oil

    3 Eggs

121. Chocolate beetroot cake, image https://www.goodto.com/recipes/beetroot-chocolate- cake

180°C or fan 160°C or Gas Mark 4

Mix all the dry ingredients together in a large bowl.

Cook the beetroot in the microwave. Or, a small amount of water in with the beetroot in a casserole dish works well. Let the beetroot cool.

Peel the beetroot and put in a liquidiser - blitz well.

Gradually add the eggs and then the oil to the liquidiser.

Pour into the dry ingredients and mix/ fold in gently with a spoon.

Pour into a deep cake tin and bake.

Cook for forty-five minutes. Check to see if cooked. I find it usually takes longer, but every oven is different.

It is a very moist, rich chocolate cake - small portions are advisable ... Enjoy

Roffey allotment site today

It is good to speak to a new plot holder to see what their experience is like, and so in 2022, I spoke to Shamim Ahmed who took on his plot last September having been on the waiting list for a year and a half. Shamim has been in this country for six years and Horsham for three, having come originally from Bangladesh. He has a wife and a two-year old son who occasionally accompanies him to the plot.

Shamim started clearing his plot in February and March and is aware that he has consequently been a little late in planting out his tomatoes, squash and other vegetables. Impressively, he works on the plot for a couple of hours each day. He says he loves gardening and helped his father when he was a teenager, he also had a roof garden at some point and grew flowers. He is finding the UK weather a little difficult to figure out as it is different to what he is used to and he is trying to grow Asian vegetables. However, when I looked around his plot everything looked very healthy and well-tended. There were some excellent chillies, courgette, tomatoes, spinach, radish, and strawberries which were still producing. He has an interesting way of growing Asian squash, lifting them above the ground on a canopy.

He has found Roffey plot holders very welcoming and he was given plants such as tomatoes to get him going as he was late with seed sowing. There has also been lots of advice and he now knows to cover the soil in winter with weed suppressant and to start seed sowing early in Spring. It's a steep learning curve for Shamim but he clearly loves it and is a hard worker.

122. Shamim Ahmed on his plot.

123. Shamim's method of growing squash.

Allotment Refuge

The Arun goes rogue,
bursting banks, reclaiming
flood plains, thieving topsoil,

careering down roadsides.
Patiently I cut the old canes
and string away from the wires,

the frame that held their harvest.
The allotment quietly thrums
after the rain, air vibrating.

I disentangle the new canes,
tying, looping, securing.
Its peaceful here, birds sing.

I think of Australia, its fragile
native landscape still burning.
I cut down the raspberry canes

confident of new spring growth,
harvest Jerusalem artichokes
and kale, untouched by flood or flame.

Chapter 14: *Shelley Allotments*

124. Entrance from Redford Avenue onto the Shelley allotments.

Shelley is a large site of about seven acres. Many of the original ten rod plots (250m2 or 0.025 ha) are now split into five and three rods, with perhaps only twenty per cent remaining as ten rods. There are about 135 renters on about 160 plots. A couple of plots had been given over to extra space for the track in and out from Redford Avenue and Saxon Crescent. Plot rents are due from the end of March each year and the whole site is leased from the Council, originally for a period of twenty-one years to 2011, until Neil Chapman, the previous Chairman, negotiated an increase of up to twenty-five years.

Improvements to the site were made in the early 2000s thanks to an energetic committee led by Neil Chapman. A small brick building, originally provided by the council with a chemical toilet, was converted into two plumbed toilets with the help of funding from the Allotments

125. Entrance from Redford Avenue onto the Shelley allotments.

126. The community wooden building.

127. Chickens on an allotment plot.

Regeneration Initiative. This initiative also contributed to improvement of the water supply and there is now piped water to seven water tanks. These do not have taps but are fifty-gallon dipping tanks which Arthur King helped to maintain by making lids for them.

At the top of the allotment site, near the Saxon Crescent entrance and the boundary row of large oak trees, land has been given over to a community wooden building with veranda. Again, with the help of the Initiative money, this replaced a previous wooden storage shed. It is now a good community space where vegetables can be left and swapped, and in the past barbeques were held. Somewhat surprisingly for Horsham allotments generally, on one plot there are chickens, just a few, well fenced and in fine feather.

From the archives

The Shelley Allotment Society is probably one of the oldest allotment societies of all the Horsham town allotments sites. There is evidence of very successful annual shows held in August each year, displaying vegetables and flowers. The first one was held in 1901 and their twenty-third show was held at Springfield Park in 1924. A later one in 1929 was held at Horsham Park, only a year after the park had been acquired by Horsham Urban District Council. However, the present Society and site were founded in 1948, as the following story from the archives explains.

On the 5th February 1942, the Sussex Daily News suggested that the Shelley Allotment Society had been functioning for over fifty years, which would take it back to the 1890s. It featured in the papers because the allotmenteers had been evicted from their plots by the council for new housing and had to be provided with alternative sites, but this was proving more difficult than first thought. It is uncertain where exactly they were originally, but a letter from the council in reply to a critical article in the West Sussex County Times in September 1946 mentioned that the old Shelley allotments were at the back of Shelley Road. This land, nine acres, had been purchased by the developers, Davis Estates Ltd. Some allotment holders had been compensated but with the outbreak of war the land was re-occupied by the council while alternative sites were sought.

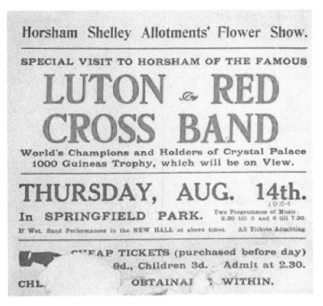

128. Poster for Horsham Shelley Allotments Flower Show on 14th August 1924 with a visit by the Luton and Red Cross Band. Horsham Museum poster archive. 1998.1226.

One alternative site might have been the old brickyard not far from the original allotments. This land was being sold by Messrs J & S Agate Ltd., for £3,450. The district valuer had a look and offered £3,000 but the finance committee thought they could apply for a grant for it to be used as a playing field and recreation ground so this is what happened.

The council had offered the Shelley Allotment Society alternative land at Hills Farm with the co-operation of the existing tenant, Mr Collins. It had been used apparently for many years by approximately ninety plot holders and could be extended, but they would have to relinquish the land as the cemetery would expand in time. In any case the society refused as it was felt to be too far away to be a proper alternative allotment site for Shelley.

Before the outbreak of the second world war in September 1939, the council had been negotiating with the Davis Estates to jointly purchase thirty-three acres of Spencer's Farm which had come up for auction the previous year. At this point Spencer's Farm was owned by the trustees of W Prewett of the stone flour mills in Horsham. The Davis Estate agreed with the council that for £5,870 it would buy twenty-three acres for its own building development and offer the council ten acres for allotments. The trustees wanted a better price and so negotiated some more and eventually both parties settled for £6,235, plus fees, £4,735 from the Davis Estate and £1,500 from the council, so the deal was agreed. However, it was all halted by the outbreak of war and the farm was understood to be re-let on a short tenancy.

Post war the negotiations continued but the council discovered that Spencer's Farm had not been re-let but had been sold to a relative, not one of the trustees, a Mr CG Prewett, who was living in the old farmhouse and did not want new houses around him. Another relative also now owned one of the fields and was living on-site in a caravan. More negotiations were undertaken by the council and in November 1945, it was agreed that the council would buy the farm for £7,000, plus fees, and agree to fence and make clear the boundaries. Also agreed was the purchase of Trinity Field for £1,500, to the south of the area designated for public green space. They also talked of building a communal hut for the allotments and installing water. The council applied for a loan of £9,602 to cover all these expenses from the Ministry of Health, which was granted and so various alternative plans were drawn up.

129. Plan of Spencer's Farm to be auctioned in 1939. WSRO UD/HO/21/2/198.

130. Council plans from 1944 with differing amounts of land for housing and allotments. WSRO UD/HO/21/2/199.

Access to any allotments needed to be negotiated and for a number of years the idea of widening the strip of a footpath next to, what was then, 72 Kempshott Road was discussed with the owner, but it remained a footpath, vehicular access later being arranged from Redford Avenue. Also, the negotiations were underway for the removal of hedgerows, the cutting down of fifteen oaks and one ash, plus the blasting of tree roots on the allotment site.

Different developers were considered for the *housing of the working classes* or council housing, on the Spencer's Farm land. Initially the urban council thought of 113 houses and eight bungalows, but it was criticised for not keeping pace with demand, as there were 770 families on the waiting list. The council was also being heavily criticised for not providing the pre-war agreed replacement allotments for the Shelley Allotment Society.

By 1948, the area of allotments being proposed had shrunk from seven acres to 1.38 acres which was an oval area between Redford Road and Saxon Crescent with the suggestion of twenty-seven, five rod plots with a fee of ten pence per rod per annum. However, by May 1950, the surveyor had laid out thirty-eight plots and twenty-two were already allocated. Unfortunately, this plan was not kept in the archives, but the increase in the number of plots suggests that the council may have had a change of heart and the oval area put aside for council housing, now Eyles Close and the allotment site shifted back to its current location.

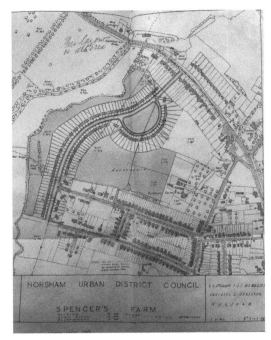

131. Council plans from 1944 with differing amounts of land for housing and allotments. WSRO UD/HO/21/2/199.

A number of different developers built small quantities of varying styles on the Spencer's Farm site for the council: Rowland Bros built eight houses, Messrs Hoad & Taylor built ten, SA Gregory built twelve, J Longley & Co. built fifteen, Cook & Sons twelve, and TJ Lovell & Son fourteen. Davis Estates was going to build twelve but pulled out and these were built by Higgins & Edwards Ltd. All the housing appeared complete by 1950, and, in fact, there were complaints

132. The footpath to Shelley allotments today from Kempshott Road.

from the Shelley Allotment Society that children from the new housing estate were making a playground of the allotment site, and one person's new cloches had been stolen. The society were asking for fencing and gates.

It seems that by this time demand for housing was declining and an interesting article appeared in the West Sussex County Times, 20th January 1948. Headed, Free Allotments, it stated that Davis Estates were offering their undeveloped building land to be used as temporary allotments. The Horsham Urban District Council Allotments Committee said it was a, 'Wonderful offer.' and that the allotments would be free to those who applied to the Davis Estates. The committee said it would let the Shelley Allotments Society know of the company's offer. It is not however clear where this land was, and if it was taken up by Shelley, given that they had their seven acres from the council. Or perhaps this was all part of that decision to increase the allotment site from 1.38 acres to seven acres in 1948?

133. Council plan from 1948 showing housing in pink, 15.17 acres, allotments in yellow 1.38 acres and open spaces in green, 8.47 acres.

In a rather worrying development of history repeating itself, Shelley Allotment Society was alarmed to receive a letter from Horsham District Council on 29th November 1985, informing them that the site had only been temporary since 1946 and so the council did not intend to renew the lease but would take back the allotment land for housing development and offer an alternative site on the edge of town. Shelley Allotment Society swung swiftly into action consulting with the National Society of Allotment and Leisure Gardens (NSALG), going through the archives and getting the local paper, neighbourhood council and residents on their side. In February 1986, at a meeting with the council, the society presented evidence that the current site was classified as statutory allotments and not temporary. The council had to accept this and withdrew their outline planning application.

Remembering the past

There appear to be few structures; sheds, greenhouses or polytunnels. This was due to quite strict rules in the past against such structures. Large outdoor boxes were used instead to store individual plot holders' tools. Plot holder, Doreen Kerr who has a lovely magnolia on her plot, can remember back to the 1950s being pushed by her dad in a wheelbarrow up to the site; presumably one could not even leave wheelbarrows up there.

Today, there is not quite such a ban against sheds and tools, although glass in greenhouses is discouraged for safety reasons. Brenda King remembered when there was a ban against growing flowers, although clearly this is not the case today. She also spoke of a plot holder who had planted fruit trees with the intention of selling his fruit, which was of course against all allotment rules and so the chap took his trees and moved on.

Arthur King remembered talk of developers wanting to push through from Collingwood Road, taking down the bordering oaks, and presumably meeting Saxon Crescent. Thus splitting the allotment site in two and allowing one side to be developed with houses. The evicted allotmenteers were to be offered plots at Rookwood. However, the story goes that a councillor's house looked out onto the allotments and he did not want a new vista of housing, so it did not happen.

134. Arthur and Brenda King on their allotment.

A recipe: Rebecca's Salsa Verdi

This is a recommended recipe for Salsa Verdi from Rebecca Johnston, Secretary of the Shelley Allotments Society. Rebecca kindly spent time telling me all about the allotment site, as well as the tomatillos that she grows on her allotment. Apparently, tomatillos are the traditional fruit to use for salsas.

135. Rebecca Johnston's tomatillos.

1. Pick the tomatillos – they should fill their paper case when ready to pick
2. Remove the paper casing and wash in warm water – they are slightly tacky to the touch when first picked.
3. Put on a baking sheet with onions garlic and chillies (to taste) I just pour a little olive oil over them.
4. Bake in the oven for about 40 minutes until they are all squishy. De-seed the chillies if preferred and squeeze out the garlic.
5. Put everything into the food mixer and give a whizz until all blended.
6. I serve with tortilla chips or crispbreads – delicious!

136. Salsa Verde, image: https://pixabay.com/photos/pesto-tomatoes-meal-food- healthy-1776673/

Shelley allotment site today

Rather than a newsletter as there used to be, there is now a website allowing people to check for allotment news, the rules and regulations and codes of conduct and to contact the committee. There is also space for a blog. The information on the website makes clear there is a committee of nine volunteers running the society and two independent trustees. Like most other societies it is a member of the National Society of Allotment and Leisure Gardens. The current chair is Ed Coulson who I was able to speak to briefly, and who has lots of exciting plans for the future.

There has clearly been a move towards *no dig* gardening with some raised beds among chipped bark paths. The chipped bark is delivered to anyone who wants to use it, which is most helpful for keeping paths free of weeds and mud. Many are now keen to move towards organic gardening which benefits the local wildlife.

Before the 2020 pandemic there were regular coffee mornings with seed and plant swaps. There was a summer barbeque with raffle prizes and an annual Autumn Show with prizes for a number of different categories. In October there was a Pumpkin Competition with more prizes and refreshments. In November each year was the AGM and again more awards for best newcomer, most improved plot and best plot. The best plot took the Shelley Cup, which was quite an achievement.

137. No dig beds on Shelley Allotments.

With the Covid pandemic beginning to lift, there are new plans that the committee have in store for Shelley allotments. They intend to change their bonfire plot and possibly two more, into a relaxation and remembrance garden which is a lovely idea so that older people and those on their own can sit and talk with others, or just contemplate the world. Another plan is to establish a community allotment, which will encourage local people to have a go at growing without the immediate commitment of a whole plot, which can be a bit overwhelming. Community plots also have the advantage of being friendly, allowing shared stories, garden tasks and produce. It may be possible to get local schools involved.

Following a better understanding of the importance of pollinators and the loss of wildlife over the last few years, the committee is starting to seed wildflowers and native plants in the verges and drainage ditches surrounding the allotments. There will be more encouragement to harvest rainwater and harmful chemicals will be banned. There are suggestions for starting a seed swapping circle where locally collected seed is exchanged. Beehives may also be introduced. Shelley allotments have lots of plans to enhance the site and make it truly inspirational for the plot holders and their families.

Painting 10. My allotment shed, by Dr Maggie Weir-Wilson

Conclusion

It is clear that Horsham town has an impressive provision of large and small allotment sites which are of increasing value to the community as time progresses. Horsham was an early adopter of allotment plots through the Horsham Labourers' Friend Society and then the council, who in the war years designated a number of allotment sites. One hopes that future councils will appreciate what a precious legacy they have in these sites and resist the temptation to sell them for development. However, given that they are all statutory sites, and given the increasing demand for plots, this seems unlikely at present, but appeal is always open to a government sympathetic to building.

As has been seen in my description of each active site, they are all subtly different according to size, and how the individual society committees run each site. Some sites are quite social while others less so. Although I was researching and writing about them during, and just after, the Covid pandemic so perhaps this was more difficult to assess? There is no doubt, however, that allotmenteering does bring people together. There is a camaraderie on the plots that is fun, helpful and reduces isolation. You can always get help and advice with your crops. I was impressed that there were groups of volunteers on most sites who were prepared to cut grass and trim hedges, clear neglected sites and do anything necessary to maintain good order.

Another delightful aspect of these allotments is the diversity and sometime quirkiness of plot holders. One could see experiments with the solar powering of irrigation, water features and kettles, an Asian way of growing squash on platforms, carrots growing in a bath, beautiful Italian heritage tomatoes, and a plot full of grapevines. People learn from each other and try things out, sometimes it works, sometimes it doesn't, but it's all interesting and goes to build the community.

It was noted by many older allotmenteers that there are fewer rules these days with regard to structures and what you can grow on your plot. Sheds, greenhouses and polytunnels are common on sites now, although there are some communal ones which seem a good idea. Flowers, once forbidden, are now encouraged as they bring in pollinators and are more sustainable than shop bought flowers.

A new development in response to climate change, and the loss of insects due to the overuse of pesticides, is the establishment of wildlife areas. These are plots, which are often in the shadow of trees and hedges and thus difficult to manage, which are set aside and managed to attract wildlife. Also, on individual plots, people have been creative in building bug houses and mini-ponds to welcome wildlife.

Environmental concerns are foremost in the minds of allotmenteers who have to cope with whatever the weather throws at them. Gale force winds blow down polytunnels, long hot summers play havoc with growing beans, and then there is watering – endless watering. We know that no dig cultivation retains soil health by not disturbing all those microscopic beasts and bacteria that make and move nutrients to our plants. We know that covering the soil when not growing crops with weed suppressant, cardboard or green manures retains the carbon in the soil, and so all these techniques are increasingly being used, and encouraged on allotments now.

Another gradual change that is evident on our Horsham allotments is the increasing number of women that are taking on allotments. Within living memory, it was always men who delved and dug, bringing home their produce for the women to prepare and cook. Now it is the women who rent almost half of the

138. A Chesworth allotment in all its summer glory.

plots on our allotment sites, and families are introduced to this activity as well. Involving children in the production of food and learning about the wildlife is hugely important for the future, so I was delighted to see two schools thoroughly involved with their own plots on two sites.

In addition to the youngsters, it is encouraging to see some plot holders still going strong well into their eighties, something I aspire to. There is no doubt that home grown organic produce, straight from the plot is good for you. That is quite apart from the continuing exercise which sustains muscle, balance and general mobility. More recent research has suggested that also being out in nature, surrounded by green plants and trees, lifts one's mood and lowers anxiety.

So, what is not to love about our Horsham town allotments? They are a valuable amenity that does so much good for both plot holders and planet. That is why I wanted to record them for posterity, long may they continue and prosper.

Bibliography

Buchan, U. (2014) *A Green and Pleasant Land*, London: Windmill Books, The Random House Group Ltd.

Burchardt, J. & Cooper, J. (eds.) (2010) *Breaking New Ground, nineteenth century allotments from local sources*, Milton Keynes: FACHRS Publications.

Burchardt, J. (2002) *The Allotment Movement in England, 1793-1873*, Woodbridge, Suffolk: The Boydell Press.

Clevely, A. (2006) *The Allotment Book*, London: HarperCollins Publishers Ltd.

Foley, C. (2010) *The Allotment Source Book*, London: New Holland Publishers (UK) Ltd.

Foley, C. (2014) *Of Cabbages and Kings, The History of Allotments*, London: Frances Lincoln Ltd.

Goulson, D. (2019) *The Garden Jungle, or Gardening to Save the Planet*, London: Vintage, part of Penguin Random House Group Ltd.

Goulson, D. (2022) *Silent Earth, Averting the Insect Apocalypse*, London: Vintage, part of Penguin Random House Group Ltd.

Griffin, C.J. (2014) *Protest, Politics and Work in Rural England, 1700-1850*, Basingstoke, Hants: Palgrave Macmillan

Gurney, J. (2013) Gerrard Winstanley, *The Digger's Life and Legacy*, London: Pluto Press.

Hammond, J.L. & Hammond, B. (1911, 1995) *The Village Labourer 1760-1832*, London: Longman Group Ltd.

Leslie, K. & Short, B. (1999) *An Historical Atlas of Sussex*, Chichester: Phillimore & Co. Ltd.

Rebanks, J. (2020) English Pastoral, *An Inheritance*, UK: Allen Lane, part of Penguin Random House Group.

Riley, P. (1979) Economic Growth, *The Allotments Campaign Guide*, London: Friends of the Earth.

Sexton, K. (2011) *Minding My Peas and Cucumbers, Quirky Tales of Allotment Life*, Chichester: Summersdale Publishers Ltd.

Short, B. with May, P., Vines, G., Bur, A-M. (2012) *Apples & Orchards in Sussex*, Lewes: Action in Rural Sussex and Brighton Permaculture Trust.

Smith, D. (2013) *The Spade as Mighty as the Sword*, London: Aurum Press Ltd.

Stuart-Smith, S. (2020) *The Well Gardened Mind*, London: William Collins, imprint of HarperCollins Publishers Ltd.

Todd, A.C. (1956) An Answer to Poverty in Sussex 1830-45, *The Agricultural History Review,* Vol 4, No. 1 pp. 45-51.

Walton, T. (2007, 2008) *My Life on a Hillside Allotment*, Corgi Books, part of Random House Group Ltd.

Way, T. (2008, 2012) *Allotments*, Oxford: Shire Publications Ltd.

Willes, M. (2014) *The Gardens of the British Working Class*, New Haven and London: Yale University Press.

Illustrations

Illustration

Index

Page numbers in bold refer to illustrations

Foley, Caroline 35
Food rationing, 1940 30, 32
Ford, Janis 133, **133**
Forest Law 18
Friends Allotment Committee 31
Friends of the Earth 36
Fry, R & Co 98

G

Gale, Leigh Ann 7
Garden Organic 37
General Enclosure Act, 1845 26, 28
George V, King 29
George, Lloyd 29
George Pinion Court 62, 63, **63**, 64
General Strike 30
Gibson, John 81
Gilbert, Davies 23
Gilbert, Mary Ann, Mrs 23, 24
Gilissen, Nero 128, **129**
Gloucestershire 21
Gorings Mead 71, 72, 74
Goulson, Dave 37
Great Reform Act, the 22
Graylingwell Park 39
Gregory SA 145
Grub Street 106
Guildford Road 64
Guinea Gardens 27

H

Hammond, Sue 66
Harris MP & Co, Builders Merchants 62
Harrison, Christina 136
Harrison, John 39
Harwood House 116, 134,
Harwood Road Allotments 51, 113, **113**, **116**, **117**, **118**, 119
Heneghan, Peter 53

Henry Doubleday Research Association 37
Hepworth, Andy 82
Hepworth's 78, 82
Heritage Seed Library 37
Higgins & Edwards Ltd 145
Highwood Village 40, **40**
Hill, Christopher 18
Hills Cemetery 120, 121, **121**, 122, **122**, **123**
Hills Farm 121, 123, 143
Hills Farm Allotments 8, 15, **41**, 64, 73, 121, 122
Hills Farm Allotment Society 122
Hills Parkland 121
Hoad & Taylor, Messrs 145
Hogg, Robert 87
Honeysuckle Walk 135
Hornbeam Close 53
Horsham Allotment Gardens 94
Horsham Burial District Joint Committee 122, **122**
Horsham District Council (HDC) 5, **41**, 51, 63, 71, 76, 87, 91, 93, 122, 135, 146
Horsham District Parks Department 5, 7
Horsham in Bloom 31, 75, 76, 137
Horsham Labourers' Friend Society 14, 24, **24**, 25, **25**, 26, 94, 134, 151
Horsham Museum 7, 13, 24, **24**, **74**, 75, **108**, 113, **122**, **143**
Horsham Organic Gardeners 37
Horsham QEII School 54
Horsham Rural Parish Council 43, 44, 114
Horsham Union Workhouse 25, 134
Horsham Urban and Rural District Council 122

Roffey and District Allotment Society 107, 134
Roffey Post Office 134
Rowland, Mr 29
Rowland Bros 145
Royal Assent 30
Royal British Legion Housing Association 62, 63
Royal Horticultural Society 32, 38
Rudridge 84
Rural Rides 21
Rushams Road 59, 61, 62, 64, **64**, 65
Rusper Road 125, 127, 128
Russell, Mark **80**, 81

S

Salter-Smith, Heather 136, **137**
Saxon Crescent 141, 142, 145, 147
Second World War 32, **33**, 35, 96, 109, 135, 143,
Seekers 18, 19
Sexton, Kay 39
Shaw, Ian **72**
Shelley allotments 61, 74, 123, 141, **141**, 143, 145, 146, 148, **149**
Shelley Allotments Society 61, 142, 143, 145, 146, 148, 149
Shelley, Sir Timothy 22
Shepheard, Frances 121
Siney, Alan 25
Small Holding and Allotment Act, 1908 26
Smith, Charlie 60, 61, 62, 65
Smith, Mr 75, 89
Society of Bettering the Condition and Increasing the Comforts of the Poor (SBCP) 21
Society of Friends, see also Quaker Movement 20, 30, 31
Soil Association, the 37

South East allotment site, Horsham 25
Southern Water Authority 85
Spade is mightier than the sword, the 32
Spencer's Farm 143, 144, **144**, 145
Springfield Park 59, 60, 63, 142
Stallibrass, Peter 56
Star allotment site, Horsham 25, 134
Station Yard 78
St George's Hill 18, 19, 20,
St Johns Close 96
St Leonard's Forest 4, 21, 106
St Mary's Graveyard 122
Strawford Centre 105
Subterranea Britannica **80**, 81
Sussex 17, 20, 21, 22, 23, 52
Sussex Area of Federated Allotment and Horticultural Societies 31
Sussex Daily News 142
Swindon 31
Swing Riots, the 21, 23

T

Tanyard Close 96
Tewson, John 78, 82, **82**
Thomas, Tim 81
Thorns, Liz 78
Thorpe, Harry 167
Thorpe Report, 1969 32, 35, 89,
Tithe map, 1840, 14, 25, 26, 93, 106, 127, 134
Tolpuddle Martyrs 23
Tomatillo 148, **148**
Trafalgar Road, Horsham 25
Transition Horsham 38, 84
Tree, Isabella 37, 38
Trinity Field 144
Tull, Jethro 20

I hope you've enjoyed reading Growing Together – Horsham's Town Allotments. If you have the time, I would appreciate your review on Amazon, Goodreads and on your social media platforms. Please share my book's cover with your social media review.

We are fortunate to have an abundance of green spaces surrounding Horsham and my book entitled, *St Leonard's Forest: A Landscape History* is a study of one of these spaces which you can buy from local shops or borrow from our Sussex libraries. The story of how I came to write this forest book follows on the next page. I also write blogs and articles about the history and landscape of Horsham district, which are on my website www.maggieweirwilson.co.uk

Very best wishes,

Dr Maggie Weir-Wilson

St Leonard's Forest, West Sussex: A Landscape History

When I began to research my landscape history thesis on the forest, I discovered that little had been written specifically about St Leonard's Forest. It became increasingly clear that its boundaries were lost in time. Control over the forest was complex and changing, and recorded information, that I could view, was limited.

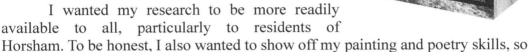

However, six years later with a lot of perseverance and encouragement, I was awarded my doctorate at the University of Sussex.

I wanted my research to be more readily available to all, particularly to residents of Horsham. To be honest, I also wanted to show off my painting and poetry skills, so I have included them in the book as well! I have distilled the research into this book which I am now delighted to launch into the world.

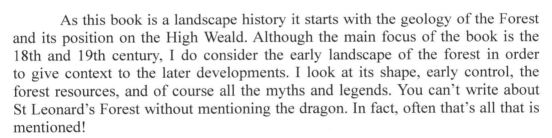

As this book is a landscape history it starts with the geology of the Forest and its position on the High Weald. Although the main focus of the book is the 18th and 19th century, I do consider the early landscape of the forest in order to give context to the later developments. I look at its shape, early control, the forest resources, and of course all the myths and legends. You can't write about St Leonard's Forest without mentioning the dragon. In fact, often that's all that is mentioned!

I follow with themes of Industry and Agriculture, then Routeways and Trade, before looking at the main forest estates and how their owners' ideas and interests in horticulture impacted on the parks and gardens in their part of the forest landscape. I look at the two villages of Colgate and Lower Beeding, the churches and its people according to the local 19th century census, which will interest family historians.

I finish by taking up the theme of Society and Community within the forest.

In the Final Word, I offer the hope that others might take up the challenge to research and write about St Leonard's Forest. There is lots more that could be explored, like the natural history and biodiversity, or perhaps historical comparisons with other Wealden Ridge forests. I do hope you will buy my book, enjoy reading it, and find out some things you may not have known, and of course be inspired to walk its footpaths.

Ingram Content Group UK Ltd.
Milton Keynes UK
UKHW050304280323
419244UK00004B/34

9 781838 343668